Splunk Developer's Guide

Second Edition

Learn the A to Z of building excellent Splunk applications with the latest techniques using this comprehensive guide

Kyle Smith

PUBLISHING

BIRMINGHAM - MUMBAI

Splunk Developer's Guide
Second Edition

First published: May 2015

Second edition: January 2016

Production reference: 1190116

Published by Packt Publishing Ltd.
Livery Place
35 Livery Street
Birmingham B3 2PB, UK.

ISBN 978-1-78588-237-1

www.packtpub.com

Credits

Author
Kyle Smith

Reviewer
Marco Scala

Commissioning Editor
Veena Pagare

Acquisition Editor
Vinay Argekar

Content Development Editor
Amey Varangaonkar

Technical Editor
Taabish Khan

Copy Editor
Trishya Hajare

Project Coordinator
Suzanne Coutinho

Proofreader
Safis Editing

Indexer
Hemangini Bari

Graphics
Abhinash Sahu

Production Coordinator
Shantanu N. Zagade

Cover Work
Shantanu N. Zagade

About the Author

Kyle Smith is a self-proclaimed geek and has been working with Splunk extensively since 2010. He enjoys integrating Splunk with new sources of data and types of visualization. He has spoken numerous times at the Splunk User Conference (most recently in 2014 on *Lesser Known Search Commands*) and is an active contributor to the Splunk Answers community and also to the #splunk IRC channel. He was awarded membership into the SplunkTrust as a founding member. He has published several Splunk Apps and add-ons to Splunkbase, the Splunk community's premier Apps and add-ons platform. He has worked in both higher education and private industry; he is currently working as an integration developer for Splunk's longest running professional services partner. He lives in central Pennsylvania with his family.

I'd like to thank my wife who most graciously put up with all my BS during the writing of this book. Without her, this effort is meaningless.

About the Reviewer

Marco Scala has been working for more than 15 years delivering solutions to large enterprise customers, first in the APM and J2EE fields and, since 2009, in the fields of operational intelligence and Splunk. He has provided consultancy for big Splunk installations for major customers, focusing on the best and most effective solutions for each different customer's needs. Since 2012, he's also a certified Splunk trainer.

In the last few years, Marco's major focus has been to get Splunk customers to gain the maximum value from their IT data and provide the business a better view and insight. Big Data is another major field of interest, and his next challenge is using Splunk to give customers useful insights and a practical implementation and exploitation of Big Data.

www.PacktPub.com

Support files, eBooks, discount offers, and more

For support files and downloads related to your book, please visit www.PacktPub.com.

Did you know that Packt offers eBook versions of every book published, with PDF and ePub files available? You can upgrade to the eBook version at www.PacktPub.com and as a print book customer, you are entitled to a discount on the eBook copy. Get in touch with us at service@packtpub.com for more details.

At www.PacktPub.com, you can also read a collection of free technical articles, sign up for a range of free newsletters and receive exclusive discounts and offers on Packt books and eBooks.

https://www2.packtpub.com/books/subscription/packtlib

Do you need instant solutions to your IT questions? PacktLib is Packt's online digital book library. Here, you can search, access, and read Packt's entire library of books.

Why subscribe?

- Fully searchable across every book published by Packt
- Copy and paste, print, and bookmark content
- On demand and accessible via a web browser

Free access for Packt account holders

If you have an account with Packt at www.PacktPub.com, you can use this to access PacktLib today and view 9 entirely free books. Simply use your login credentials for immediate access.

Instant updates on new Packt books

Get notified! Find out when new books are published by following @PacktEnterprise on Twitter or the *Packt Enterprise* Facebook page.

Table of Contents

Preface

Splunk is awesome. Not only can you consume virtually any data with it, you can also extend and integrate Splunk with virtually any external system. Splunk uses sets of configurations that are referred to as applications or add-ons, which is the primary focus of this book. Leveraging these applications and add-ons is what gives Splunk its unique ability to extend, learn, analyze, and visualize information.

Splunk helps users to determine the root cause of a failure, a quick overview of system health, and dive deep into SQL statements and messages, just to name a few. The aggregation and centralization of log and event management is a growing trend in the Big Data space. By leveraging the combined intelligence gathered from correlating disparate sets of data, businesses or individuals can make data-based decisions. This book will help a Splunk developer, or even just a curious end user, to develop different methods of consuming new data, design new types of visualization, or even just offer tips and tricks that help the software development lifecycle.

Overview of what this book isn't

Most developer guides will tell you what their book is and/or does. We aim to explain what this book isn't, and allow you to fill in the rest with your imagination! Thus, proceed to this list:

- Will not cover Splunk basics
- Will not cover creating dashboards via the GUI (other than HTML)
- Will not discuss how to code in Python
- Will not discuss statistics
- Will not cover SDKs
- Will not discuss making beer

Splunk basics will not be covered. These include concepts such as searching (finding data, using timecharts, stats, some eval commands, and so on), reporting (making basic pie charts or line charts via the GUI), data inputs (basic file monitoring, TCP and UDP inputs, Splunk forwarders, and so on), and configurations (GUI and web-based configuration editing), to name a few. Creating dashboards via the GUI? Nope. Python will be discussed and sample code will be provided, but this book will not cover the nuances of the code, nor will it teach you Python syntax. We will not cover statistical computation, other than how to practically apply some basic math to create value-based visualizations. We will not cover using the SDKs (software development kits) being used in custom Splunk applications that are external to Splunk (for example, Angular, PHP, .NET, and others). These are out of the scope of this book. Free as in beer? Nope, the choice of hops, starch, and oak-barrel aging for the creation of beer will not be discussed, but rather consumed during the writing and/or reading of this book.

 Unless otherwise stated, this book uses Splunk version 6.3 as the development environment.

What this book is

This book will guide you through many the different areas of Splunk App and add-on creation. We will start by looking at the design aspects of an App or add-on, how to create them, what knowledge objects are available for use within the App, ways to enhance your App with metadata and external data, and some basic views and dashboards. From there, we will move into the Splunk Web Framework, modular inputs, jQuery, web framework programs, and then packaging and publishing Apps and add-ons. At the tail end, we will highlight some areas of the Splunk community that prove to be very useful.

Assumptions

There are a few basic assumptions that we are going to make. Having purchased or otherwise obtained this book, we assume that you are interested in developing with Splunk, and have a basic understanding of Splunk and how to navigate around the software. Knowledge of saving searches, reports, and basic dashboarding is a must, since most concepts and examples will be built upon the basics. We also assume that you have basic knowledge of HTML, CSS, JS, and some XML. Here, XML will be limited to the Splunk XML framework specifically. We would also recommend you to have knowledge of, or proficiency in, Python, RequireJS, and other web technologies such as Bower, npm, and Gulp. We will demonstrate how to use these web technologies within a Splunk application.

What this book covers

Chapter 1, Application Design Fundamentals, discusses fundamental questions and considerations before diving into an App or add-on configuration.

Chapter 2, Creating Applications, discusses the basic methods of App and add-on creation, along with an explanation of the structure of an App or add-on.

Chapter 3, Enhancing Applications, discusses a few different configurations that help to enrich your data with Splunk knowledge objects, along with some basic App and add-on branding guidelines.

Chapter 4, Basic Views and Dashboards, goes through the basics of SimpleXML dashboard creation and development.

Chapter 5, The Splunk Web Framework, details the various SplunkJS Stack components and shows examples of how to use them within an HTML dashboard.

Chapter 6, Advanced Integrations and Development, reviews modular inputs, data models, the KV Store, and modular D3 visualizations.

Chapter 7, Packaging Applications, lists the items needed to package an App or add-on, in order to get it ready for publishing.

Chapter 8, Publishing Applications, explains step by step how to upload an App to Splunkbase, and includes some information on the great support community.

What you need for this book

To take full advantage of all the examples and code contained within this book, you should have the following items:

- An installed and running instance of Splunk.
- Basic knowledge of how Splunk works, including searching, basic panels, and dashboards.
- An understanding of the various technologies that Splunk uses. These include the following:
    - Python
    - JavaScript
    - HTML
    - CSS

Who this book is for

This book will benefit both the casual Splunker and the experienced professional alike. Whether you are just starting Splunk Apps or add-on development, or have been developing for years, this book has tips and tricks to help with developing new integrations and Splunk Apps and add-ons. Even for quick modular input, this book provides quick tutorials on common integration techniques and code examples.

Conventions

In this book, you will find a number of text styles that distinguish between different kinds of information. Here are some examples of these styles and an explanation of their meaning.

Code words in text, database table names, folder names, filenames, file extensions, pathnames, dummy URLs, user input, and Twitter handles are shown as follows: "Copy the file to $SPLUNK_HOME/etc/apps."

A block of code is set as follows:

```
[splunk_developers_guide]
coldPath = $SPLUNK_DB\splunk_developers_guide\colddb
homePath = $SPLUNK_DB\splunk_developers_guide\db
thawedPath = $SPLUNK_DB\splunk_developers_guide\thaweddb
```

Any command-line input or output is written as follows:

```
cd $APP_HOME/default
```

New terms and **important words** are shown in bold. Words that you see on the screen, for example, in menus or dialog boxes, appear in the text like this: "Simply click on the **Browse** button."

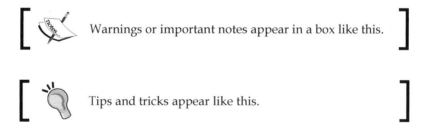

Warnings or important notes appear in a box like this.

Tips and tricks appear like this.

Reader feedback

Feedback from our readers is always welcome. Let us know what you think about this book—what you liked or disliked. Reader feedback is important for us as it helps us develop titles that you will really get the most out of.

To send us general feedback, simply e-mail feedback@packtpub.com, and mention the book's title in the subject of your message.

If there is a topic that you have expertise in and you are interested in either writing or contributing to a book, see our author guide at www.packtpub.com/authors.

Customer support

Now that you are the proud owner of a Packt book, we have a number of things to help you to get the most from your purchase.

Downloading the example code

You can download the example code files from your account at http://www.packtpub.com for all the Packt Publishing books you have purchased. If you purchased this book elsewhere, you can visit http://www.packtpub.com/support and register to have the files e-mailed directly to you.

Errata

Although we have taken every care to ensure the accuracy of our content, mistakes do happen. If you find a mistake in one of our books—maybe a mistake in the text or the code—we would be grateful if you could report this to us. By doing so, you can save other readers from frustration and help us improve subsequent versions of this book. If you find any errata, please report them by visiting http://www.packtpub.com/submit-errata, selecting your book, clicking on the **Errata Submission Form** link, and entering the details of your errata. Once your errata are verified, your submission will be accepted and the errata will be uploaded to our website or added to any list of existing errata under the Errata section of that title.

To view the previously submitted errata, go to https://www.packtpub.com/books/content/support and enter the name of the book in the search field. The required information will appear under the **Errata** section.

Piracy

Piracy of copyrighted material on the Internet is an ongoing problem across all media. At Packt, we take the protection of our copyright and licenses very seriously. If you come across any illegal copies of our works in any form on the Internet, please provide us with the location address or website name immediately so that we can pursue a remedy.

Please contact us at copyright@packtpub.com with a link to the suspected pirated material.

We appreciate your help in protecting our authors and our ability to bring you valuable content.

Questions

If you have a problem with any aspect of this book, you can contact us at questions@packtpub.com, and we will do our best to address the problem.

1
Application Design Fundamentals

Hello there, Splunk developer! If you are like us, we know you have a love of Splunk and all of the endless possibilities that present themselves! The Big Data world is exploding around us, and it always feels like a tireless battle when keeping up to date with advances in technologies, platforms, and concepts. Here, we will discuss none of those. This book is dedicated solely to Splunk and the development of applications for Splunk. Onward and upward!

What is a Splunk application?

All that being said, let's talk Splunk applications. A Splunk application is nothing more than a structured set of configurations and assets used to achieve an end goal of data collection, indexing, and visualization. Furthermore, in order to create a valid Splunk application, you must include the ability to navigate. Without navigation within the application, you would be working on an add-on. According to Splunk, applications:

- *Contain at least one navigable view*
- *Can be opened from the Splunk Enterprise home page, from the App menu, or from the Apps section of Settings*
- *Focus on aspects of your data*
- *Are built around use cases*
- *Support diverse user groups and roles*
- *Run in tandem*

- *Contain any number of configurations and knowledge objects*
- *Are completely customizable, from frontend to backend*
- *Can include Web assets such as HTML, CSS, and JavaScript*

 This is taken from `http://docs.splunk.com/Documentation/Splunk/latest/AdvancedDev/AppIntro`.

Why applications?

Applications allow us to quickly share configurations, focus on the context of available data, limit data access to specific individuals or groups, and organize similar dashboards and views into a cohesive presentation of data within Splunk. Sharing applications can be as easy as just zipping it up and sending it out. Splunk applications could be said to be *open source*, due to the fact that almost all of the configurations, custom scripts, and any other knowledge object contained within the applications, are readable on the filesystem. This allows for customization for an individual instance while maintaining an overall *master configuration*.

Definitions

To get started, we should define a few *naming conventions* typically used when naming applications. Note that while we will use these naming conventions as the best practice, your application can really be named anything at all, which may conflict with other applications of the same name, or violate Splunk usage agreements or publishing guidelines. In particular, the name *Splunk* cannot be present in your application or add-on name. Additionally, in the past, Splunk has referred to add-ons as *technology add-ons*, and has since moved to just *add-ons*. The following list of add-on types is our way to distinguish the different uses of each add-on:

- **Applications**: Applications could be named anything, as long as they are relevant to the content of the application and don't contain the name *Splunk*.
- **Domain add-ons (DA)**: Domain add-ons are not full applications, rather they contain the visualizations and presentation of the data for a broader application. No other configurations should be included (extracts, tags, event types, macros, line breaking configurations, and so on). Dashboards and views are the primary objects contained within this type of add-on.

- **Supporting add-ons (SA)**: Supporting add-ons are also not full applications; these contain *data definitions*, such as macros, saved searches, event types, and tags. These describe how to correlate the data, normalize the data, and consolidate the data to be usable in the domain add-on.

- **Technology add-ons (TA)**: Technology add-ons provide extraction, data massage, and index-time configurations. These can also be referred to as technical add-ons. These contain the configuration options required to properly break events, extract search fields, and create timestamps, among other functions. These are the building blocks for the SA and DA add-ons, as well as full-blown applications.

 Follow the Splunk application design guidelines. Using a custom naming scheme may cause conflicts.

Thus end the *official* naming conventions as normally seen in a Splunk installation. We will now discuss some other naming conventions that have been found to help in the wild west of various Splunk installations. These two naming conventions are of the author's own design, which have helped in some of his deployments:

- **Input add-ons (IA)**: Input add-ons are just that—configurations that assist in the collection of data, known as inputs. These add-ons are most likely found on a deployment server and are used to collect data from universal forwarders. One of the advantages to splitting your IAs from your TAs is a reduced size in the add-on being sent to the universal forwarder. This is especially useful if your TA contains lookups that aren't needed on the universal forwarder but are several megabytes in size.

- **Admin add-ons (ADMIN)**: This add-on is a very special add-on. It would typically contain *administrative* configurations that might be needed in a variety of locations. Such configurations could be the web server SSL port, deployment client information, or anything in `web.conf` or `server.conf` format. It can be used to send index information to a set of non-clustered indexers, or possibly to scale the addition of more search heads by setting all relevant settings from a central location.

While this may not be a complete list of naming conventions, it should be enough to recognize any that are seen in the wild. An additional aspect of the naming conventions that we recommend is the addition of company information. This will help your Splunk admins differentiate between Splunk add-ons and custom add-ons. Just as an example, let's say you built a TA for Cisco, specific to your company (the ACME company). Splunk's provided add-on is entitled *TA-cisco*, but you don't want to modify a vendor's offering. So, your new add-on's name could be *A-ACME-TA-cisco*. This gives you two things: an easy-to-see custom TA that relates to Cisco and the ability to override any *TA-cisco* settings based on application precedence.

Let's discuss application precedence for a moment. Splunk uses a *merged configuration* when applying configurations that are installed via the applications. The methodology that Splunk chose to implement conflict resolution is pretty simple. There are two different methods of precedence. The first is directory structure. If you have an input located in the `default` folder of an application (more on `default` in the later chapters), you can place a matching configuration in the `local` folder of the application to override the `default` configuration. The same method is applied to the applications themselves. Splunk uses the ASCII values of the names to determine precedence. On *nix, you can sort the applications in the `apps` folder of Splunk using the `LC_COLLATE=C ls` command. This will show you the ASCII-sorted order of the applications, and the first in the list will be highest priority. A has a higher priority than Z, but Z has a higher priority than a. So, the A at the beginning of the add-on name gives your add-on the highest precedence, so you can override any setting as needed.

 From this point forward, both Splunk applications and add-ons will be referred to formally as Apps purely as a convenience.

Designing the App

So you've decided that you need an App? Congratulations! Now that you know that you need one, you need to decide on a few more items as well. It is important to do a little bit of planning, as even the simplest Apps can evolve into super-complicated Apps, with dashboards, saved searches, workflows, and more. Never assume "well, this'll just be a quick development", as, most of the time, it is not.

Identifying the use case

First and foremost, try to determine the scope of your App. Once you have the scope planned out, try to limit the amount of scope creep that occurs, if possible. You may just be trying to perform extractions on your data, and if that is your current end goal, stop there. Don't try to build a full-blown suite on your first attempt. Build the IA, then the TA, and then move on from there. Ask yourself these questions as you try to determine your scope:

- What am I trying to accomplish? Search-time extractions? Index-time parsing? Dashboards to share?

- What users need access to my App? Everybody? Specific roles?

- What kind of information will I be presenting? Server based? Metric based?

- Who is my target audience? Business users who don't understand Splunk **Search Processing Language (SPL)**, or technical users who will notice that I didn't convert MB to GB properly?

These questions can help you spark an idea of what internal resources would need to be engaged, as well as any kind of documentation and educational requirements.

Identifying what you want to consume

Once you have determined the scope of the App, you will need to decide how and from where you will consume the data. Getting data into Splunk can happen in a very wide variety of ways. There is no set manner of input that will work on all data sources. You may have to develop a new script or modular input. Being aware of where your data is coming from is the key to getting it consumed correctly the first time. A few questions you may ask yourself could be:

- Why do I need this data? Is it all completely relevant to my use case?

- Where is the data? Cloud, SaaS provider, internal network?

- How do I get the data? Do I already have a collector script, or do I need to engage an internal resource to write a collector/modular input?

- What format is the data? Is it already extracted (or well known, like syslog), or do I need to write custom extractions?

There is a lot of data out in the wild, but not all of it may be relevant to your use case. You may find that of a service that has 100 endpoints available for data collection, you only need 10. Not only will you save on license usage, but your indexers will thank you for it as well.

Identifying what you want to brand

Another key thought process in App development is how far you want to brand your App. Splunk has a very robust architecture and framework, providing you with the ability to customize your Apps extensively. You can override any individual piece of CSS and extend SplunkJS Stack to include any number of different visualizations or third-party libraries. Additional questions you might ponder on would include:

- Do I want to brand anything at all, or just stay with native Splunk?
- Do I need to engage an internal graphics resource to design and create App icons? App logos?
- Am I going for mobile or static desktops? What desktop size is typical of incoming users?
- To what extent should I customize my App? Do I just change a few colors using native Splunk options or do I override CSS?
- Do I need to engage a web designer to build custom CSS or HTML layouts?

There are so many options available to brand your App, but all customizations should conform to the Splunk branding guidelines for developers. Visit `http://www.splunk.com/view/SP-CAAAFT9` to read through Splunk's guidelines.

Identifying what you want to display

Once you have the whats and hows of the data you're going to collect, you need to figure out visualizations. How you display the information is just as important as what data you collect. Splunk comes with a variety of graphs and displays right out of the box, and can be extended quite easily to include some really cool presentations. Some of the questions posed to you might be:

- Do you need a programmer to write custom modules or extend SplunkJS views and managers?
- What third-party graphing or graphic libraries do you need to document, develop, or get permission to use?
- Do you need to engage a statistician to determine the best and most effective way to display your data? Some stats (such as max, mean, and min) are easy, others (such as confidence intervals and trendlines) are not.

Such a small list of questions hardly precludes any other relevant discussion within your organization. The more internal discussion that can take place, the better and more thought-out your App may turn out.

Installing Apps

As a Splunk developer, you should be aware of the three methods to install Apps. There are advantages and disadvantages to each method, but no required method. It is mostly personal preference as to which method is used by the end user, but, typically, newer Splunk users will use the Web interface, while advanced users will use the command line. Let's review those methods, just to keep them fresh in your mind.

Splunk Web

Installing Apps via Splunk Web is simple. Once you have downloaded the App from its source, you navigate to the **Manage Apps** section of Splunk. You will find this at the top-left of Splunk Web, as shown in the following screenshot:

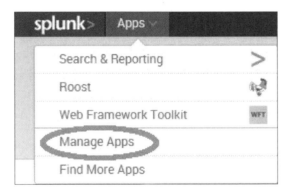

Once you have clicked on **Manage Apps**, you will see a button to install the app from a file. You can also browse the Splunk App store, using the first button:

This brings you to a form that you can use to actually install the App. Simply click on the **Browse** button, select the file you downloaded, check the **Upgrade** button if this App has already been installed, and then click on **Upload**. That's it! Splunk takes the App, installs it, and prompts to restart if needed:

The Splunk command line

CLI holds a special place in many *nix admins' hearts. It is entirely possible to install Apps via the command line alone. Doing so requires having the following: access to the physical (or virtual) server and enough permissions to perform CLI commands with Splunk. All commands are going to be executed from $SPLUNK_HOME, which normally defaults to /opt/splunk. Follow these steps to install an App via CLI:

1. Copy the App file (either a *.tgz or *.spl file) to the filesystem.
2. Run the ./bin/splunk install app <path_to_file> command.

Splunk will install the App. You may be prompted to restart, depending on the contents of the App. Index-time configurations require a restart, whereas search-time configurations do not.

Unzipping using the command line

The final methodology is to perform an unzip/untar. If the App was constructed properly, the only steps you need to perform are as follows:

1. Copy the file to $SPLUNK_HOME/etc/apps.
2. Change the file extension from .spl to .zip.
3. Use your favorite utility and unzip the file into the folder.

Caution! This will overwrite any other settings you have configured, including local configurations (if present in the zip file). We will cover directory structure in the next chapter.

 Downloading the example code
You can download the example code files from your account at http://www.packtpub.com for all the Packt Publishing books you have purchased. If you purchased this book elsewhere, you can visit http://www.packtpub.com/support and register to have the files e-mailed directly to you.

Summary

In this chapter, we covered the basic fundamentals of designing and installing Splunk Apps. Apps can be broken down into *domains*, each with a naming convention that allows you to quickly determine what the App can do, and what is contained within it, so that new users to your environment don't have to look for configurations. We learned how to approach App design to make sure that the App is planned beforehand, which will eliminate the need to refactor major portions of the App later, when it may already be in production. We also went over the three different methodologies available to install Apps to give a basic understanding of user experience related to the installation of any App you may build.

Now that you've acquired an understanding of what an App consists of, in the coming chapters, we will discuss creating, enhancing, and customizing them.

2

Creating Applications

In this chapter, we will begin covering how to build an actual application. There are many different ways to create an App, ranging from GUI creation to manual editing of configuration files. We will cover the structure of an application, what each folder should contain within the application, and why this is important. Another aspect that will be touched on will be the data that your application will consume. Setting up the data structures beforehand may save you time and energy later on if you have to refactor. It is crucial to get the data in correctly the first time, as any subsequent release of your app will need to make use of the data. We will cover various methods for data consumption, as well as the types of Splunk knowledge objects that can be included in your application. Restricting access to your application may be a priority, so we will also cover metadata and object permissions. Getting your application installed may require your end user to perform some additional configuration before it can be used, so we will review how to configure the setup screen as well.

A brief clarification

As we continue to progress through this book, we will create an App from the ground up. The App's name is *SDG* (from a filesystem perspective) and the App *label* will be *Developer's Guide for Splunk*. It will be available in its entirety on Splunkbase at `https://splunkbase.splunk.com/app/2693/`. Additionally, we will be using an API provided by **meh.com**, a *daily deal site* that was kind enough to build an API to their website. They were chosen primarily because they fit the geek culture pretty well, and provide a very simple-to-consume API. The data that will be consumed is pulled from their website's API using scripted inputs located in the `bin` folder of the sample *SDG* application.

Let's recall the questions from *Chapter 1, Application Design Fundamentals*, that revolve around App creation. We should answer some of them in preparation for building our demo App:

- Identifying the use case:

    ○ We are building this App as a learning experience for the reader. By providing an App at the end of this book, with all the examples from the book contained within the App, we will give you a means to see a final product, as well as how it was created, step by step.

    ○ We are building an App with visualizations and modular inputs that will be shared with everybody — no need for role-based access.

    ○ The data will primarily consist of daily deals information, along with polling information.

- Identifying what you want to consume:

    ○ The data is needed as an *event generator* for our App building demo, and is located at an API provided by meh.com. I will consume the data with a modular input from the API, which outputs its data in JSON.

- Identifying what you want to brand:

    ○ For demonstration purposes, we will brand the App with custom icons and some custom CSS and JavaScript. No external resources will be needed.

- Identifying what you want to display:

    ○ We will be using a box plot graphic, which needs to be transformed into a modular Splunk JavaScript library. The statistics will be simplistic, so a mathematician is not required.

Now that we have answered some preliminary questions, we are ready to begin creating our App. We can clearly see what is needed at the very basic level, and can continue to add to the specification as we go ahead.

Methods of creating applications

There are two basic ways of creating applications. They are as follows, in order of difficulty (not that any of them are hard): **Splunk Web** (we will call this the **GUI**), and **handwritten** (henceforth to be recognized as **FreeForm**). In order to create Apps, you, the developer, must have specific permissions within the Splunk instance.

Pro tip

Set up a brand new instance of Splunk with a dev license to make sure that you have all the proper permissions to develop an App.

For the GUI method, the user must be an admin within Splunk; additionally, for the FreeForm method, the user must have server access to the command line with as many permissions as required by the user that runs Splunk.

GUI

We will start with the GUI method. This is the simplest of the methods, since access to this feature can be granted via an external authentication system (if authorization is configured within the Splunk instance), or with the built-in role-based access measures. The first step is to log in. Once you've logged in to your development instance, you need to navigate to the **Manage Apps** section. Once you are inside the **Manage Apps** dashboard, there will be button that says **Create app**:

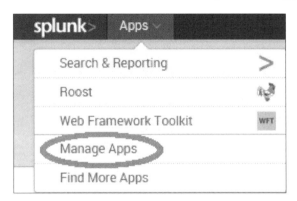

Once this button has been pressed, you will be taken to the **Create app** manager page. This page contains a form with the attributes required to start an App. For the rest of this book, we're going to use the sample App *SDG* and, from there, we will build the entire App:

The following screenshot shows the **Create app** form. Each field has a description below it that provides information pertaining to that field. This allows you to fill in the form quickly and efficiently. If you are planning on releasing this App into the wild on Splunkbase, be sure to maintain consistent version numbers (`http://semver.org` has a good specification on versioning). Another *gotcha* is the **Visible** toggle. If you are writing an App that will extract data, input data, or otherwise show no forms of dashboards or data visualizations, select that as **No**. This will prevent users from being confused when it shows up in the Apps menu list.

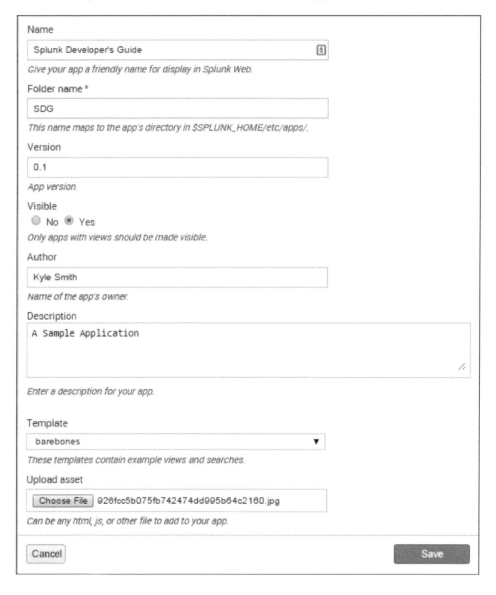

The **Template** drop-down menu will be either the **barebones** or **sample_app** option. The barebones template will create a very basic structure, with the fewest configurations required to support an App. The sample_app template generates some sample configurations (searches, views, and other knowledge objects) inside the generated app. In most cases, you will want to use barebones, as using the sample_app template will require you to delete the generated searches, extractions, inputs, and visualizations, and it is not intended for distribution. You can also upload assets using this form (but more can be added later). Once your form is complete, hit **Save**. Your App will be generated, and placed in `$SPLUNK_HOME/etc/apps`. This is the default location for Apps. The `$SPLUNK_HOME` (which defaults to `/opt/splunk` on *nix and `C:\Program Files\Splunk` on Windows) is typically your installation directory, but will vary depending on where you specify the installation to be performed. The default folder structure will be created under the folder name you provided on the form (we'll cover more on that later).

CLI

You may be wondering, "Can I create an app via the command line?" The answer to this question is, Yes! As of Splunk version 6.3, Splunk has the ability to create an App via the CLI. The command is `$SPLUNK_HOME/bin/splunk create app APP_NAME-template TEMPLATE_NAME`, where `APP_NAME` will be the name of the app you want to create, and `TEMPLATE_NAME` will be either `barebones` or `sample_app` (as mentioned earlier).

FreeForm

Another method of creating Apps is FreeForm, otherwise known as *by hand*. This is where you can navigate to the `$SPLUNK_HOME/etc/apps` folder and create the folder structure and configurations directly, through a text editor of your liking, whether that be Vim, Emacs, or Notepad. An App contains at least a minimal structure of folders and files in order to be functional, so it is suggested to keep a template copy of your App in hand. By keeping the template copy in hand, you can quickly build new Apps using the base template, and speed up development without having to recreate all of the different configurations, and risk mistyping the configurations. The following list shows the configurations and folders required for an App:

- `$APP_HOME/default/app.conf`
- `$APP_HOME/local`
- `$APP_HOME/metadata/default.meta`
- `$APP_HOME/default/data/ui/views/*.xml`

The only difference in the requirement for an application versus an add-on is the exclusion of the $APP_HOME/default/data/ui/views/*.xml files. Without dashboards and views, an application is reduced to an add-on.

Let's step through creating a basic App by hand, shall we? Of course, that's why you bought the book, unless you like conversational coffee books or beer coasters!

The $SPLUNK_HOME refers to the installation folder of your Splunk. In this case, it will be on a *nix system, at the default location. Therefore, references to $SPLUNK_HOME will refer to /opt/splunk.

The $APP_HOME refers to the App folder that you will be creating. This is located under the $SPLUNK_HOME/etc/apps folder.

So here we go! Please take note of the following caveat.

The author of the book works primarily in *nix world, so all commands and editing will be done via the CLI on a *nix machine. Non-*nix users can use the Windows GUI to implement pretty much the same concepts. The Windows command will also work for those who wish to use it.

Let's start! Follow these steps:

1. Change the directory to the Splunk Apps folder:

   ```
   cd $SPLUNK_HOME/etc/apps
   ```

2. Create a folder for the *SDG* App:

   ```
   mkdir SDG
   ```

3. Create the default folder:

   ```
   mkdir SDG/default
   ```

4. Edit the app.conf file:

   ```
   vi SDG/default/app.conf
   ```

5. Add the following content to `app.conf`:

```
## SDG Application app.conf
[install]
is_configured = 0

[ui]
is_visible = 1
label = Splunk Developer's Guide

[launcher]
author = Your Name
description = A Sample Description
version = 1.0
```

6. Create the `local` folder:

```
mkdir SDG/local
```

7. Create the `metadata` folder:

```
mkdir SDG/metadata
```

8. Edit the `default.meta` file:

```
vi SDG/metadata/default.meta
```

9. Add this content to `default.meta`:

```
## Application-level Permissions
[]
access = read : [ * ], write : [ admin, power ]
export = system
```

That's it! These are the very barebones of the App, providing only the smallest amount of configuration required. We will use this as a starting point, and continue adding configurations throughout the book.

Now that we've walked through creating the App via the two available methods, we will take a quick peek at the folder structure to give a point of reference for the definitions of the structure. The App *Splunk Developer's Guide* was created through the GUI, and has the following structure:

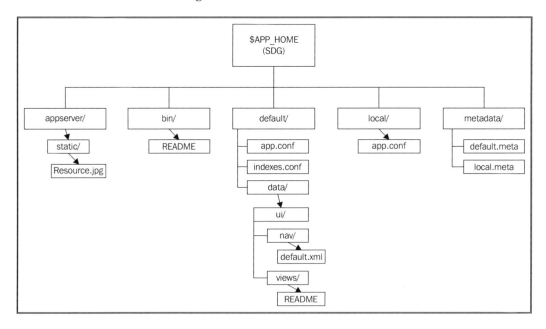

Basic application structure

Now that the App has been created, let's take a look at some of the folders that were created, what they may contain, and how they are used with the App. The folders we are going to look at come from the App that was created via Splunk Web.

appserver

The `appserver` folder contains configurations and other files that relate to some of the inner-workings of the App. In extremely advanced Apps, additional modules and MVC controllers (controllers provide the link between you and the system) are inserted into this folder. For the purpose of this book, we will focus on the `static` directory, which contains the JavaScript, CSS, and other assets required by the App.

bin

The bin folder contains *binary* assets, such as those used for modular inputs, scripted inputs, or custom commands. These are most likely Python files, shell scripts, or PowerShell scripts.

default

The default folder contains all the *App publisher's* configurations and views. When packaging Apps for publishing, you should move any configurations from your local folder to the default folder. This will help prevent overwriting any local changes that the end user might make to the configurations. This folder also contains the default navigation and dashboard files.

local

The local folder contains all the *end user* configuration and view changes that are made. App developers should not publish Apps with configurations in this folder, as they may overwrite changes that the end user has made.

lookups

The lookups folder contains all the CSV files that are used as lookups in your configurations. As a general principle, as an App developer, you should include only those lookup files that won't change. These are lookups such as HTTP status codes, or Windows Event ID lookups. Including lookups that are generated from saved searches is not good practice, as when you deploy an updated App, the lookups that were generated from the end users' data will be overwritten.

metadata

The metadata folder houses the permissions for the App. All Splunk knowledge objects have permissions as to who can view, edit, and use the objects, and these permissions are contained in two files in the directory: default.meta and local. meta. The default.meta file contains the basic options, as the App developer wants to control the permissions. The local.meta file allows the end user to change the permissions to be suitable for their environment.

static

The static folder has the static assets used by the App. This folder contains the App icons, which are displayed on Splunkbase, as well as inside Splunk in the App's menu.

Application data

Now that we have created a new App, we can start working on how we need our data indexed. Typical Apps may contain configurations for their own indexes, source types, and other input methods.

Indexes

Indexes are very useful in a new App as they allow you to physically separate the data on the disk on the indexers. This helps speed up searches and optimizes macros and event types, since only a smaller subset of data will be searched within the App. The configurations of the indexes are in the indexes.conf file, in the default folder. For our App, let's add an index. The configuration looks like this in the indexes. conf file, located at $APP_HOME/default/indexes.conf:

```
[splunk_developers_guide]
coldPath = $SPLUNK_DB\splunk_developers_guide\colddb
homePath = $SPLUNK_DB\splunk_developers_guide\db
thawedPath = $SPLUNK_DB\splunk_developers_guide\thaweddb
```

That's it! Defining indexes is a quick way of optimizing your App's data. You can also create indexes using the GUI. To make sure that you are configuring your index within your App, ensure that you are within the context of your App. To *be in context* of an App only requires you to navigate to your App in the Web interface. Once there, click on the **Settings** menu and then on the **Indexes** manager:

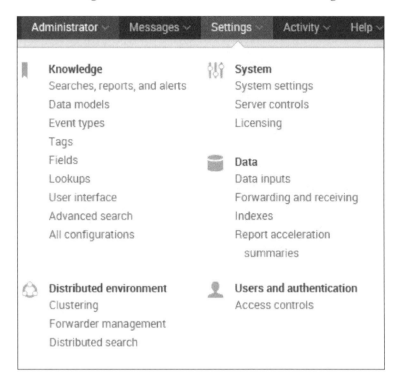

Locate the **New** button, and click on it to go to the setup page. Once there, you will fill in any required fields (the index name being the only required field) and update any others to match your environment. This is shown in the following screenshot:

Index settings

Index name *

_Set index name (e.g., INDEX_NAME). Search using index=INDEX_NAME._

Home path

_Hot/warm db path. Leave blank for default ($SPLUNK_DB/INDEX_NAME/db)._

Cold path

_Cold db path. Leave blank for default ($SPLUNK_DB/INDEX_NAME/colddb)._

Thawed path

_Thawed/resurrected db path. Leave blank for default ($SPLUNK_DB/INDEX_NAME/thaweddb)._

Max size (MB) of entire index

500000

Maximum target size of entire index.

Max size (MB) of hot/warm/cold bucket

auto

_Maximum target size of buckets. Enter 'auto_high_volume' for high-volume indexes._

Frozen archive path

Frozen bucket archive path. Set this if you want Splunk to automatically archive frozen buckets.

Cancel   Save

Once you've created the index, you can start adding data to it. A full restart of Splunk is not needed for the index to be active.

Once you have created the index, move the configuration from the `local` folder to the `default` folder, and sanitize any special path names (remove all special characters or custom locations). This will help end users with the installation of your App.

Source types

Source types are important within an App because they allow quicker searching, since they are an indexed field. If the scope of your Splunk App is a certain technology (TA) or customer use case (such as the application management of some custom application) and you have to analyze, provide KPIs, and so on, then source types will be a great focus to work on with your App.

If you are developing your App for a specific technology, then naming source types to match your App is a good idea, as this will help reduce any conflicts with existing source types when your App is installed on an end user's environment. This also allows you to break down the incoming data into specific groupings, contained within your App, and gives a finer level of control to the App developer. In general — this is a guidance, not a requirement — the proper format for naming source types related to a technology is *vendor:product:feature:format*. For example, let's say the vendor that we are developing for is Cisco. We are using their **Access Control Server (ACS)** with TACACS logging enabled. The proper source type for this data input would be *cisco:acs:tacacs*. Source types should always be lowercase in order to keep things consistent.

Sources

Sources are a field for the place from which the data is collected. Sources are identified within an App's inputs, which are generally controlled by the App developers.

Available Splunk knowledge objects

There are many different **Splunk knowledge objects (SKOs)** that can be used within an App. The only required SKO for an App is the addition of views that can be displayed to the end user. We will briefly cover the different types of SKOs that you can include within your App. To avoid any issues with *author interpretation* of the definitions of these SKOs, we will use the definitions and references from the official Splunk documentation.

Macros

noun

A parameterized portion of a search such as an eval statement or a search term that can be reused in multiple places, including saved and ad hoc searches, and which is used in a manner similar to a search command. Search macros can contain arguments, but they are not required.

This is taken from `http://docs.splunk.com/Splexicon:Searchmacro`.

Macros are configured through the **Advanced Configuration** section of the GUI, or via the `macros.conf` file located within the App. They are advantageous by allowing bits of SPL to be used as code, and can even be parameterized to make them usable in a variety of situations. They are also very useful for building dashboard searches, as a dashboard needs to be refreshed (when editing from the command line or Notepad) when the searches change, but the macros do not. Therefore, you can rapidly build dashboards by referencing macros and then editing the macros quickly.

Event types

noun

A type of knowledge object that enables you to categorize and label all the indexed events that match a specified search string. An event type has a name and an associated search.

This is taken from `http://docs.splunk.com/Splexicon:Eventtype`.

Event types are configured through the **Advanced Configuration** section of the GUI, or via the `eventtypes.conf` file located within the App. They are very useful for classifying types of data, such as *authorized login* or *failed login*, based on a Splunk search. The assigned event types for any data that you search for within the search bar are displayed as a field to the left-hand side of the search results area.

Tags

noun

A knowledge object that enables you to efficiently search for events that contain particular field values. You can assign one or more tags to any field/value combination, including event types, hosts, sources, and source types.

 This is taken from `http://docs.splunk.com/ Splexicon:Tag`.

Tags are another way of enriching, normalizing, and segregating data. They allow you to classify data across different source types, sources, hosts, event types, and so on. They offer a very granular approach to searching data; tags are created through the GUI, or are present within `tags.conf`.

Saved searches

noun

A search a user has made available for later use. Searches can be saved as reports, alerts, or dashboard panels.

 This is taken from `http://docs.splunk.com/ Splexicon:Savedsearch`.

These are particularly useful, especially when used in conjunction with macros and dashboards. A saved search can be shared among team members, can be used repeatedly within a dashboard, and can be used externally from Splunk via the API (for example, Tableau uses saved searches as part of its connection). Saved searches can also be used in dashboards, which allow the dashboard to be loaded quickly by using the saved search artifacts from the last run. This prevents massive load when multiple users load the same dashboard at the same time. Saved searches can be created through the GUI, or by editing `savedsearches.conf`.

Dashboards

noun

A type of view associated with an App. A dashboard contains one or more searches that display data in visualizations. Panels in the dashboard contain the visualizations.

This is taken from `http://docs.splunk.com/ Splexicon:Dashboard`.

Dashboards are critical to Apps, as they show all the data visualizations that are relevant to an App. Without dashboards, your App is an add-on. Dashboards have a specific place within the App, and this will be discussed later.

Lookups

noun

A knowledge object that enables the addition of fields and related values to search results based on field matching with a CSV table or a Python script. For example, you can use a lookup to perform DNS or reverse DNS lookups on IP addresses or host names in your data.

This is taken from `http://docs.splunk.com/ Splexicon:Lookup`.

Lookups help to enrich your indexed data with *static data* or *state data*. You can use Splunk to generate a *state* of your hosts, applications, and so on, and place them in a lookup file. This allows quicker loading of a *state* dashboard. Lookups are in the `lookups` folder of the App, and are generally CSV files.

Configurations

noun

A file (also referred to as a conf file) that contains Splunk configuration information. Splunk writes configuration settings into configuration files. Configuration files are stored in a number of directories, including $SPLUNK_ HOME/etc/system/default (these are preconfigured and not to be edited), $SPLUNK_HOME/etc/system/local, and $SPLUNK_HOME/etc/apps/. You can configure Splunk settings and processes by editing configuration file stanzas.

[ This is taken from `http://docs.splunk.com/ Splexicon:Configurationfile`.]

Configuration files are the meat and potatoes of your application. They decide how all of your SKOs get defined, how fields are extracted, and more. Almost everything that needs to be done can be done within a configuration file.

Object permissions

Object permissions are an integral part of securing Apps and their knowledge objects. After all, we don't want the user causing issues in an App you spent hours tweaking, do we? No, that's what I thought. This is where permissions come into play. Splunk permissions are role-based, meaning that a user needs a specific role (either assigned by Splunk or via external authentication and authorization systems) to read or write the knowledge object. Permissions are controlled within the `default.meta` and `local.meta` files in your `metadata` folder in the App, and, as per normal Splunk precedence, the `local.meta` file will override any setting with a matching stanza in the `default.meta` file.

The configuration structure within the corresponding file is as follows:

```
[<object_type>/<object_name>]
access = read : [ <comma-separated list of roles>], write : [ comma-
separated list of roles>]
```

[This structure is taken from `http://docs.splunk.com/ Documentation/Splunk/latest/AdvancedDev/SetPermissions`.]

Let's explain this a little bit. Nothing says "clear" like mud sometimes:

- `object_type`: This is the type of SKO that you are securing. Some examples are `savedsearches`, `eventtypes`, `tags`, `macros`, and `views`.

- `object_name`: This option is not required. So, if you include it, it will apply only to the URL-encoded object name, and nothing else. Omit this option and the permission will apply to all values of `object_type`. Here is an example: let's say your search name is *My First Search*. Then, this parameter will be `My%20First%20Search`. Do you see what we did there?

- `access`: You can go with this, or you can go with that. Either read or write, that is. Simply place the name of a Splunk role in a comma-separated list within brackets, and that is the person who gets to read and write the knowledge object. If a role is in neither the read nor write stanza, then the user will not have any visibility to the object.

Now, for you non-CLI folks, let's see some screenshots. You would want to start out in the area you want to modify the permissions for, which can be something such as tags, event types, or macros, to name a few. Once you have had a look at the objects you want to change, you should see the **Sharing** column, with the current permissions and a link. Click on the link.

This will bring you to the **Permissions** page for the object. Using the checkboxes and radio buttons, define the level of access you want each role to have. Leave the checkbox empty for none:

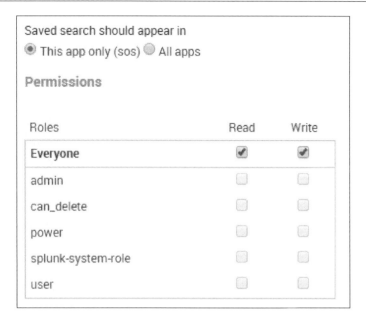

Once you have completed the configuration, click on the **Save** button, and your settings will be saved. This is how simple permissions can be in an App.

The setup screen

So let's say that your App is more advanced than some others, or that you need to have the user supply OAuth credentials to connect to a service, but you don't want them messing about in your filesystem. Oh! What to do? Well, the answer is a setup screen. Setup screens allow you to configure a form that can interact with endpoints and SKOs in your App. End users can enable or disable saved searches if they don't apply, enter credentials, or interact in a number of ways with configuration files. In the following example, we are going to first create a REST endpoint (CLI required), and then the setup file to interact with the endpoint. Allons-y!

The endpoint

First, let's see the endpoint. The endpoint we will write will be used to create and interact with a custom configuration file for our application. We will then use this configuration file later, when we create a modular input for the App. Let's do it step by step from the command line. Windows users can use Notepad and the GUI to achieve the same results:

1. Navigate to $APP_HOME/default and then execute the following command:

   ```
   vi restmap.conf
   ```

2. Enter this content:

   ```
   [admin:sdg]
     match=/sdgep
     members=conf

     [admin_external:conf]
     handlertype = python
     handlerfile = sdgHandler.py
     handleractions = list, edit
   ```

   This file controls the REST endpoint. Our endpoint will be located at `https://splunk.my.domain:8089/services/sdgep/`. Notice that the `match` parameter matches with the endpoint named `sdgep` in the URL. Next, the `members` parameter defines which other stanzas are *children* of the endpoint and can be accessed under it. The external stanza defines each handler for the endpoint (Python only, at this moment in time) and the associated actions and Python file.

3. Now, execute the following command:

   ```
   vi sdgsetup.conf
   ```

4. Enter this content:

   ```
   [sdg_config]
   apikey =
   ```

   This sets up the default configuration file for the endpoint.

5. Now, navigate to $APP_HOME and execute the following commands:

   ```
   mkdir bin
   ```

   ```
   cd bin
   ```

   ```
   vi sdgHandler.py
   ```

6. Enter the following content (this is Python, so make sure that all your indentations are correct):

```
import splunk.admin as admin
    import splunk.entity as en
    class ConfigApp(admin.MConfigHandler):
            def setup(self):
                    if self.requestedAction == admin.ACTION_EDIT:
                    for arg in ['apikey']:
                            self.supportedArgs.addOptArg(arg)

            def handleList(self, confInfo):
                    confDict = self.readConf("sdgsetup")
                    if None != confDict:
                     for stanza, settings in confDict.items():
                            for key, val in settings.items():
                                    if key in ['apikey'] and val in [None, '']:
                                        val = ''
                                    confInfo[stanza].append(key, val)

            def handleEdit(self, confInfo):
                    name = self.callerArgs.id
                    args = self.callerArgs
                    self.writeConf('sdgsetup', 'sdg_config', self.callerArgs.data)

    admin.init(ConfigApp, admin.CONTEXT_NONE)
```

7. This Python code is a simple file editor script. It will open the sdgsetup. conf file and modify it, according to the Splunk rules of precedence and default/local. The user will use a form (setup.xml) that will have the content of the file. It supports two actions, list and edit (the functions are named accordingly).

The setup file

Now that we have a custom endpoint, let's review and write the setup.xml file. The setup.xml file lives in the default folder. For now, our setup page will include only the setup for the API key that we will use later in the modular input, but keep your eyes open for updates to this file throughout the book.

1. Execute the following commands:

    ```
    cd $APP_HOME/default
    ```

    ```
    vi setup.xml
    ```

2. Enter this content:

    ```
    <setup>
            <block title="Authentication" endpoint="sdgep/conf"
    entity="sdg_config">
                    <input field="apikey">
            <label>The APIKey for meh.com api</label>
                            <type>text</type>
            </input>
            </block>
        </setup>
    ```

Let's explain this little bit of code. The `setup.xml` file must start with `<setup>`. Once that is in place, you will be able to add additional *blocks* of configuration settings, each with different endpoints and entities. In this case, the entity we want is our custom one (from the `sdgHandler.py` file). So, in this file, the `endpoint` should be the same as `match` in the `restmap.conf` file, with the additional specification of matching the member config. Thus, the `endpoint` attribute of the block tag is generalized as `endpoint/member`. The `entity` (in this case) is the stanza within that file that you wish to target, which is config in this App. The `input` tag allows you to then specify which configuration option under that stanza you want to modify. There you go—a `setup.xml` file that will prompt the user to enter an API key on first navigation to the App:

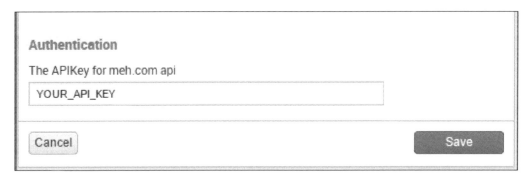

Once the user fills out this form and submits it, the App is considered to be *configured*, and the `local/app.conf` file will be updated to reflect this.

Summary

In this chapter, we looked at a few different methods of creating Splunk Apps. There are two basic methods of creating Apps: via the Web and via the CLI. We looked at the structure of the App and what each folder may contain. We also covered what kinds of objects (in a non-exhaustive list) can be included in a Splunk App. We discussed permissions, and how to assign them in two different ways. We then went over how to set up a REST endpoint to control configuration, as well as a setup screen to allow the user to update credentials within the App.

Up next, we will discuss the different aspects of enhancing your App with event types, workflows, and some acceleration techniques.

3
Enhancing Applications

In this chapter, we will focus on enhancing your App with branding elements, workflows, event types, tags, macros, data models, and more. None of these items are a strict requirement. However, they will definitely increase your appeal to end users and customers alike. Choosing elements that are memorable will cement your App in the minds of your users and will make your App shine. We will start with working with your data, and then move on from there to presenting your App with custom logos, navigation, CSS overrides, and other stock modifications of the SimpleXML dashboards. We will end this chapter by seeing how to use Splunk acceleration technologies and methods to speed up searches in large datasets. As we move into working with actual data, we will be using example data and real data. Some of the data here was consumed from the `https://meh.com/` website. They have an API, and the data was collected every five minutes using a scripted input. This data will be the basis for some examples and some dashboards that highlight various features. More important than the data is to grasp the concept. Grasp the concept; rule the software.

Workflows

Workflows integrate with your data and are designed to help you move quickly through your data, or help you to integrate easily with other services. They can be used to drill down to another Splunk dashboard with prepopulated data in the request, perform an nslookup on an IP address in an event, open a ticket in an external ticket tracking system, or even launch an external search-all based on data found within the event. Workflows are displayed inline with the events you are working with. They don't have to apply for every single event. You can restrict a workflow to be revealed only when target events are listed, or a set of fields are listed. Workflows can be configured via the Web or configuration files.

Building a workflow in the web interface is straightforward. As part of our *Splunk Developer's Guide* (SDG) App, we will create a workflow that will interface with the `http://mxtoolbox.com/` website to perform a reverse DNS lookup based on an IP address in the `src_ip` field found in some sample data. The first step is to navigate to the configuration area for workflows. This is found in the top-right corner of the screen. Navigate to **Settings** | **Fields** | **Workflows**, as seen in the following screenshot:

Fields

View, edit, and set permissions on field extractions. Define event workflow actions and field aliases. Rename sourcetypes.

Type	Actions
Field aliases	Add new
Edit or add one or more aliases to field names	
Calculated fields	Add new
Edit or add one or more calculated fields	
Field extractions	Add new
View and edit all field extractions. Add new field extractions and update permissions.	
Field transformations	Add new
Edit or add transformations for field extractions that use a transform.	
Sourcetype renaming	Add new
Rename a source type. Multiple source types can share the same name.	
Workflow actions	Add new
Edit or add workflow actions	

Click on **Workflows** to be taken to the correct manager. Now you have a form to fill in, as shown in the following screenshot. Don't we all just love paperwork? So, let's walk through it:

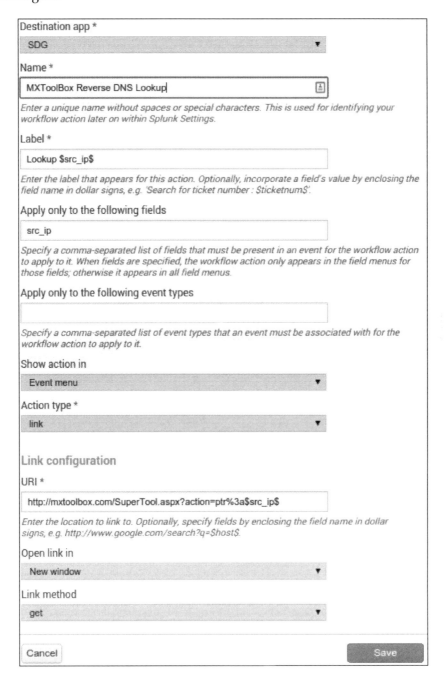

Give it a name, something descriptive. The name won't show up in the Web interface; that is the purpose of the **Label** field. In the **Label** field, you can place variables that are relevant to the data. So, for example, if you have an event with src_ip=75.75.75.75, then the **Label** will expand to Lookup 75.75.75.75. The next field details which fields are mandatory in the event in order for the workflow to be visible. Do the same for the **event types** textbox. The **Show action in** drop-down dictates where the clickable menu item will be shown. The **Action type** drop-down menu can have a link or a search option. The only time it won't be a link is when you want Splunk to perform a new search based on that data. Once those are set, you can configure the actual action. In this case, the URL we need is http://mxtoolbox. com/SuperTool.aspx?action=ptr%3asrc_ip, which will automatically expand to http://mxtoolbox.com/SuperTool.aspx?action=ptr%3A75.75.75.75 based on the sample data. Finish it off with the **New window** option and a **get** configuration, and you are done! Note that after creating the workflow, the permissions are changed to be App only, where everyone can read but only admins can write, as shown in the following screenshot:

Name ↕	Owner ↕	App ↕	Sharing ↕
MXToolBox Reverse DNS Lookup	admin	SDG	App | Permissions

Setting up a workflow via a configuration file is just as easy. Let's make a Google search for a specific field. Navigate to $APP_HOME/default and edit the workflow_ actions.conf file. Insert the following content into this file as a new stanza:

```
[Google Search]
display_location = event_menu
fields = site, topic
label = Google $topic$, restrict to $site$
link.method = get
link.target = blank
link.uri = https://www.google.com/?q=site:$site$+$topic$
type = link
```

This will do exactly what the DNS lookup workflow does, except that it is a Google search restricted to the $site$ website, as found in your sample data. This workflow will apply only to events that have the site and topic fields.

Custom alert actions

New in Splunk Enterprise 6.3, **custom alert actions** (also called modular alerts) allow a developer to define an integration that can be reused multiple times and in different ways based on the data being presented to it. Custom alert actions interact specifically with the alerts that were already present in Splunk. There are a few new components that go into making a custom alert action (let's call this a **CAA**). We will discuss the various components of a CAA and build a very simple CAA that will output the results of the search into a file within the App.

The first step in the creation of a CAA is to determine what your alert is intending to do. While it is possible for your alert to do multiple actions, do not try and combine multiple technologies unless necessary. For example, you wouldn't want to combine a Facebook action with a Twitter action, since both actions require separate authentication and authorization methodologies and credentials. Once you have narrowed the scope of your CAA, we can proceed with the very basics of a CAA. We won't dive into the full implementation of a CAA, due to the fact that Splunk has a set of really nice documentation. The full documentation of CAAs can be found at http://docs.splunk.com/Documentation/Splunk/latest/AdvancedDev/ModAlertsCreate.

For a very simple CAA, the basics that are required are as follows:

- A CAA configuration (this is stored in `alert_actions.conf`)
- A script (this is stored in the `bin` folder of the App)
- **User interface** (**UI**) definition (this is stored in `default/data/ui/alert_actions` of the App)

There are many more options available; we would suggest you read the documentation to get the full effect. Let's start with the name of our CAA. Let's call it `file_write`. Once we have our name, we will update `alert_actions.conf` to have the following information:

```
[file_write]
is_custom = 1
label = File Writer
alert.execute.cmd = caa_file_write.py
payload_format = JSON
param.res_link = $results_link$
```

Break it down now! The first line, the stanza heading, is the name of the CAA. The first attribute (is_custom) allows Splunk to know that the CAA is a custom alert, not a typical alert. The second attribute is label, which will show in the Splunk UI, so make it pretty and clear to understand. The third attribute (alert.execute.cmd) is the $APP_HOME/bin relative filename for the alert script that you are implementing. The fourth attribute (payload_format) specifies how you want to pass in data (JSON is very nice, but there are instances where XML might be preferred). The final attribute (param.res_link) is a custom parameter that will get sent to the script each time it is called.

Once you have the configuration stanza in place, you can place the script into the bin folder of $APP_HOME. Let's place the following code in a file called caa_file_write.py:

```
import sys, json, urllib2
def write_file(settings):
    f = open('myfile','w')
    f.write("%s"%json.dumps(settings))
    f.close()
if __name__ == "__main__":
    caa_config = json.loads(sys.stdin.read())
    write_file(caa_config)
```

Let's break it down. The first line is import statements. Pretty typical of Python, am I right? Then, we define a write_file function that will take the settings passed to the alert and write out the settings to a file. Then, our main code block pretty much just reads the config from the standard in, and passes it to the write_file function. Then, save it. Once we finish creating the custom alert (we need to add an HTML file first), and then create an alert, you will see a file with the settings written to it.

The user interface portion of the CAA is required in order to provide an interface for the end user to place configuration settings. This file, which should be named the same as the CAA (in this case, file_write.html), should be placed in $APP_HOME/default/data/ui/alerts. For example, let's take a look at the expected code:

```
<form class="form-horizontal form-complex">
  <div class="control-group">
    <label class="control-label" for="file_name">file_name</label>

    <div class="controls">
      <input type="text" name="action.file_write.param.file_name"
        id="file_name" />
      <span class="help-block">File name to write to (located in
        the local folder)</span>
    </div>
  </div>
</form>
```

As you can see, the UI HTML for CAAs is pretty simple. The HTML doesn't have to be a full HTML-spec page, it can be partial HTML, as long as it validates. It can also contain Bootstrap CSS classes and formatting. There are a few special bits. Located in the `input` tag above, the `name` attribute of the input correlates to the parameter name of the CAA. This allows Splunk to tie the two together, allowing custom settings. For each parameter, you would, in the same way, put the HTML into that file. Once these are in place, restart Splunk to pick up the changes. Once you have logged back in, open a search and search for anything. Save that search as an alert, choose the **File Write** alert, and give it a filename (if you wish). After that, sit back and enjoy the file on the server. Of course, this is a super easy example, and you probably would want your CAA to do something useful. It's all in your hands now. For a more technical and in-depth read, consult the documentation, as it goes far deeper into requirements for App certification.

Enriched data

Naturally, when we talk about enriched data, we are talking about separating the isotopes of our data and storing them in secure storage, right? Nope! No weapons-grade data here! The term **enriched data** refers to adding extra context to raw data. Therefore, the data is then enriched. We will now cover event types, tags, and macros.

Event types

Event types are used to classify similar events into categories. Categorizing events is important because it can help you search through a large amount of data quickly, find patterns, or create specific alerts and searches. They are defined by users via the GUI or via the command line, or they are part of a prepackaged app. Event types can have permissions assigned to them so that only specific roles can view or edit them. Defined event types will show up in the user's **Field List** during a search in the GUI and, as such, can be modified and searched just as a normal field can be. Event types are defined by a Splunk search. Let's create an event type, shall we? The data we are going to use is consumed from the meh.com API, as mentioned earlier. The data is in JSON format.

At the time of writing this section, the deal for the day was a JBL speaker dock with sunglasses. There is a running gag on meh.com that on Fridays, they only sell speaker docks. So, let's categorize this deal as `speaker_dock`. Then, as additional speaker docks are sold, we can quickly exclude only those categorized as `speaker_dock` — really, who wants a speaker dock?

There are three ways of creating an event type. The first is directly from the event. So, using our search, we pull the events into the **Events** tab. To the left of the **Time** column, there is an arrow that expands the event. Once expanded, there is a button labeled **Event Actions** with **Build Event Type** as an option:

Clicking on it will open the event type builder. Splunk will automatically try and suggest some field values for you to include as part of the event type, and will also include some sample events. At the top, you can see an **Edit** button. This will allow you to define explicitly what you want to use as the event type. Alternatively, you can use the checkboxes to the left. Each click on the textbox will regenerate the sample events list, which now matches the generated event type at the top. Since we already know that we are looking for speaker boxes, let's edit the event type to the following:

```
index=splunk_developers_guide sourcetype=meh "speaker dock"
```

After clicking on **Save**, you will get a chance to name it and set the style or priority. Then, click on **Save** again. This saves the event type in your App, as shown in the following screenshot:

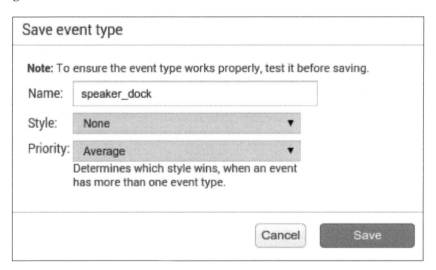

Once you have saved the event type, rerun the search and you will see the event type listed in the fields list. Clicking on that field will show you some statistics about the field values:

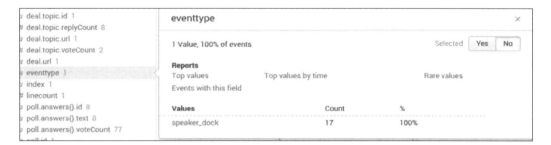

 Every event that matches that search will count as one event type of that value. So, if you are running an input every five minutes, you will have a new event type every five minutes.

A second way to create an event type is directly through the manager. Navigate to **Settings** | **Event types** and then click on **New**. Meh also has roombas (robot vacuums) from time to time, so let's create an event type for those, just in case we spot one. Once you have clicked on the **New** button, you will have a form to fill in. Fill in the details, as shown in the following screenshot, and click on **Save**. You can ignore the **Tags** field for now; we will discuss that shortly.

There is also a third option, and it is probably the most popular. Start with a simple search. Once you have narrowed the search down to only the events you want in the event type, find the **Save As** button to the right of the search bar. Click on it and choose **Event Type**:

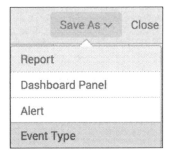

Once you select this, another dialog will pop up. Simply fill out the fields and click on **Save**:

And that is how you create event types using the web interface. The other option available is to use a configuration file (which is where the configurations from the Web are stored). The file is called `eventtypes.conf`, which makes complete sense. Here, you define the event type in the same way as you would for any other configuration. There is a stanza that holds the name of the event type, and then an attribute that holds the Splunk search that matches the new event type.

Let's create one for a Eureka vacuum. Edit the `eventtypes.conf` file by adding the following to the content:

```
[eureka]
search = index = splunk_developers_guide sourcetype = meh eureka
vacuum
```

Save the file and reload the configuration.

Whenever you edit the configuration by hand, you should reload the debug endpoint.

This is as easy as hitting a URL in a browser. The URL is `https://<yourSplunk>/en-US/debug/refresh`. Be careful—this might take a while on large installations.

You can specify which endpoint you want to refresh by adding `?entity=<entity>` to the URL, where `<entity>` is the one in the supported list. See the list simply by loading the debug/refresh endpoint. For only event types, your URL will be `https://<yourSplunk>/en-US/debug/refresh?entity=admin/eventtypes`.

Once the reload completes, navigate to the event types manager in the Web. You will see all the three event types we just created. Did you notice how the permissions are different? If you create knowledge objects via the web interface, the objects will inherit your user-level permissions. If created on the command line, the objects will inherit the default permissions for the App (located in `default.metadata`). Don't worry about this for now; those permissions will change when we package the App for publishing:

Name ⇕	Search string ⇕	Tag(s) ⇕	Owner ⇕	App ⇕	Sharing ⇕
eureka	index = splunk_developers_guide sourcetype = meh eureka vacuum		No owner	SDG	Global | Permissions
roomba	index = splunk_developers_guide sourcetype = meh roomba		admin	SDG	App | Permissions
speaker_dock	index=splunk_developers_guide sourcetype=meh "speaker dock"		admin	SDG	App | Permissions

And there we have it! Event types will help you categorize and classify your data to allow faster searching and statistics. Make them as granular or broad as your situation and App require. Now, defining event types in this manner requires that we know our own data. But, what if you don't? If the data is new to you, or is a new type of data in the environment, you can use Splunk to discover event types for you. We won't go into the details of the semantics of how to use it, but there is a command that will generate the results with some sample data and some suggested tags:

```
index=splunk_developers_guide sourcetype=meh | typelearner
```

The `typelearner` command will output a table with your data, information on existing event types, and suggested tags, which brings us to... tags!

Tags

Tags are knowledge objects that help categorize and normalize your data. Tags can be applied to any combination of the `<field>=<value>` definitions. They are particularly useful when used in combination with the Splunk **Common Information Model** (**CIM**). The CIM contains a standard set of tags and definitions that define and categorize data. Most Splunk-provided apps are CIM compliant, and any App created should also be CIM compliant.

 CIM compliant refers to the Common Information Model, provided by Splunk as a normalization technique. For more details on this, check out `https://apps.splunk.com/app/1621/`.

Tags are created in a few different ways. Splunk 6.2 allows you to create tags right from the search results, as well as with the manager. We won't revisit the manager for tags, since that is a standard methodology of creating knowledge objects (the tag manager is located at **Tags** under **Settings**). Let's instead look at how to create them from the command line and the search results. We've loaded our meh.com search results and expanded one of the events for a speaker dock. Navigating the field list shows drop-down arrows to the right of each field, since tags can work on any field-value combination. Clicking on an arrow reveals **Edit Tags**, which then opens another dialog:

eventtype ⌄	speaker_dock	⌄
index ⌄	splunk_developers_g	
linecount ⌄	1	Edit Tags

Tags can be virtually any text, with individual tags separated by commas or spaces. In this example, let's tag the event type we just created — `speaker_dock`. Firstly, we will tag it with `speaker`. This is an abstract tag that could refer to any type of speaker, not just a speaker dock. Secondly, we will tag it with `useless`, because they don't really serve a purpose. I mean really, a single place to play music?

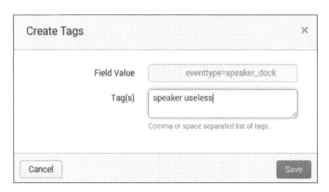

Once you have saved the tags, they will show up within the search results next to the value. This is a quick way for you to see what tags have been assigned to each field-value combination:

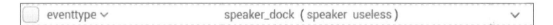

The structure in the configuration file is slightly different for tags. The stanza consists of the field-value pair, and the attributes are the tag names that are enabled. Let's take a look and make one for the roomba. A roomba is a type of robot, so let's tag it with `robot`. The configuration is stored in the `tags.conf` file. Edit that file (in the `default` folder) by adding this:

```
[eventtype=roomba]
robot = enabled
```

Don't forget to refresh the endpoint; this will pick up the change from the configuration file. Now, if you are interested in products that are robots, you can simply search for the `robot` tag:

```
index=splunk_developers_guide sourcetype=meh tag=robot
```

This search will look for any field-value combinations that have been tagged as `robot`. So, as you begin to tag more and more products, your searches, alerts, and dashboards will begin to include those items automatically.

Macros

Next up are macros. Macros are sections of reusable searches that can be used whenever a Splunk search is done. Macros can contain any part of a search, including evals, other pipe commands, or search terms. They can also accept arguments. Arguments passed can be strings or fields. If a field is passed, its value is used in the macro when it is expanded. Macros can also be *evaluation* macros. In this case, they strictly perform an evaluation and return the result as a string to the search that called it. This is useful for calculating bandwidth, for example. Macros are also useful for setting the *base search* of your App. By setting a base macro and using it in subsequent searches, reports, event types, and so on, your end users can quickly adapt your App to their environment with a simple macro update. We will create a base macro for meh.com data as an example. The manager for macros can be found by going to **Settings | Advanced Search | Search Macros**. Once you are in the manager, click on the **New** button. This brings you to a *gasp* form that you have to fill in! Starting to see a pattern? Let's fill it:

The **Name** field is self-explanatory, except when arguments are involved. When naming a macro, if you are using arguments, the name must contain the number of arguments in parentheses. For example, if `meh_base` had one argument, its name would be `meh_base(1)`. The **Definition** field is the search string subset that you want to execute when the macro is called. In this case, the macro definition points to the base data for meh.com. Simple, yeah? The rest of the fields are for an evaluation-based definition. We will define that directly in the configuration file. When you click on **Save**, then, once again, you will have successfully saved a knowledge object. You will see the saved macro in the manager. Once a macro is created, you can call it in a search object. The syntax is like this: enclose the name of the macro in backticks (`). Henceforth, this macro will be referenced as `` `meh_base` ``. That's it! The macro is expanded and added to the search you are performing.

Use the job inspector (**Activity | Jobs | Job Inspector**) to see the full expansions of macros to help troubleshoot problems.

Macros are expanded *in place*, so the position within your search will matter. The `'meh_base' earliest=@d` macro definition is different from `earliest=@d 'meh_base'`, depending on the definition of the macro. For example, if your macro contains any additional commands, you will need to place the macro after the search terms. Our second method will create an evaluation-based macro in the configuration file. This macro will take the price of the current item for sale from the consumed data and convert it into Canadian dollars (based on the current exchange rate at the time of writing this chapter) — let's face it, the Canadians are pretty cool! I mean, hockey, maple syrup, curling, and Chris Hadfield. Need I say more? Macro configurations are stored in the `macros.conf` file. Note that the definition has quotes around it. This tells Splunk to return the result as a string, which is a requirement for evaluation-based macros:

```
[mehToCA(1)]
iseval = true
args = price
definition = "$price$ * 1.24"
```

Again, don't forget to reload the configuration, since you've changed a configuration file. The endpoint for this change is `admin/macros`. Once the endpoint is reloaded, you can use it in a search, as follows:

```
'meh_base' earliest=@d | rename deal.items{}.price AS price | eval
canadianPrice = `mehToCA(price)`
```

The resulting field based on the sample data at the end of this chapter will be `canadianPrice = 22.32`. Macros are very powerful and can compress your massive 40-page-long search into a much, much smaller version, making them very simple to read and edit. By combining various aspects of data transformation and extraction within a macro, you can quickly share parts among your team, or within your App. One change to the macro and all instances using that macro will also change. One additional best practice should also be mentioned. While it is possible to place a macro into an event type, it is not recommended. The expansion of the macro in the event type is not possible in a distributed architecture, unless an additional flag is set in the configurations for the App.

Lookups

How can one overlook lookups? Lookups are just that—lookups. They can be either file-based or external scripts. They provide a means of looking up static data that is, data that doesn't change very often or is simply too massive to index continuously. For instance, Active Directory user information, HTTP status codes, Oracle action IDs and descriptions, and so on, could be in a lookup. The example lookup we are going to create will be generated from existing code. This particular lookup will be used as a *state table*. A state table is a lookup that stores the state of objects that you specify. This can be things such as port status (is it up or down?), last price (stocks perhaps), or anything that has a constantly evolving status. This will show you how to configure, read, and write a lookup. We will discuss external lookups, but we will use a built-in to Splunk, as it is often overlooked, and asked about often on `https://answers.splunk.com/`.

First, we have to decide what we are going to store in our lookup. We want to be able to quickly get statistics about products from `https://meh.com/` for the last 30 days. Searching each individual event over 30 days might take a while, especially for large datasets. So, we want to create a lookup (state table) from the existing data, and use it later in a dashboard. We won't create the dashboard now, but we will create a saved scheduled search. Let's start by defining the lookup. There are two ways to create a lookup: one via the Web and the other via configuration files. We will run through the Web interface and then we will look at the configuration file for the created lookup. Start by navigating to **Settings | Lookups**. Once there, you will see three options. If you have existing lookups, or you want to upload a new file, you should choose **Lookup table files**:

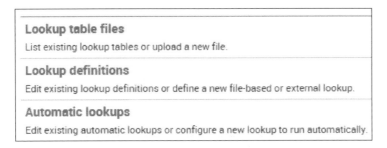

Lookup table files

List existing lookup tables or upload a new file.

Lookup definitions

Edit existing lookup definitions or define a new file-based or external lookup.

Automatic lookups

Edit existing automatic lookups or configure a new lookup to run automatically.

Automatic lookups are used to add configuration to allow you to automatically look up data based on fields in events. For example, if you are looking at an IIS log, you can automatically look up the status code description of the event and have it prepopulated in the field list. The first thing we need to do for a lookup is to create a file for the information to reside in. Click on the **Lookup table files** item and click through to the new table manager. You will have to choose a file to start with. Here, we used a simple CSV file with the following content in it:

```
product_id,product_price\r\n
```

The \r\n part shouldn't be visible. We just need to make sure that there is a line break inside the lookup file. This filename is called `meh_products.csv`:

Choose that file and give it a destination name, which should be the same as the source file name. Then, click on **Save**. This uploads the file to the filesystem and makes it available for the lookup definitions manager.

As always, we need to set the permissions to the App level so that the configurations aren't stored within the user's folder.

Now, head over to the lookup definitions manager and click on the **New** button. As with other knowledge objects, we want to make sure that we are placing them within the **SDG** App context. Give it a name — we used `meh_products`:

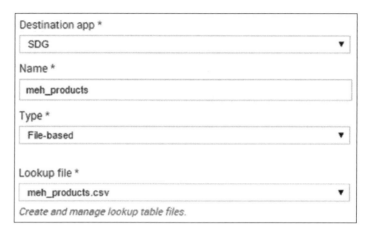

This is the name that you will use within the saved search. You will need to choose the file that you just uploaded. Then, click on **Save**. This creates and reloads the configuration for your product's lookup.

You might want to create this from the command line; it is actually pretty simple. Navigate to your `$APP_HOME/lookups` folder and then create the `meh_products.csv` file within that folder. Lookup configurations are stored in the `transforms.conf` file, so head over to the default file and place the following configuration:

```
[meh_products]
filename = meh_products.csv
```

Pretty simple, right? As far as the configuration is concerned, we have now completed that. Next, we have to use it. Firstly, we need to generate the lookup daily using the existing lookup, add new data, and then output the new data. We will show you the search first and then explain each part:

```
`meh_base` earliest=@d | inputlookup meh_products append=t | stats
latest(deal.items{}.condition) as product_condition latest(deal.
items{}.price) as product_price latest(deal.title) as product_title
latest(eventtype) as product_type earliest(timestamp) as product_
date by deal.id | rename deal.id as product_id | dedup product_id |
outputlookup meh_products
```

Let's break it down. This search is scheduled for 1:00 a.m. every day. This will cause the lookup to be generated based on when the daily deal rotates, which is every midnight:

```
`meh_base` earliest=@d
```

This section of the search uses a macro from before and then restricts the data to only the day of execution:

- ```
  stats latest(deal.items{}.condition) as product_condition latest(deal.
  items{}.price) as product_price latest(deal.title) as product_title
  latest(eventtype) as product_type earliest(timestamp) as product_date
  by deal.id | rename deal.id as product_id
  ```

This elongated `stats` command simply takes the raw JSON fields (which we are interested in collecting) and turns them into a *standard* set of fields. Note that we are using `deal.id` as the `by` clause, since that should always be unique. Then, we rename `deal.id` to be `product_id`. Much cleaner!

```
inputlookup meh_products append=t
```

This portion of the search pulls in the data that has already been saved. It is important to note the `append` attribute of the `inputlookup` command. Without this attribute set to `t` (or true), the lookup data will *overwrite* the pulled data from the first part of the search. When used as the first command in the search string, this attribute can be dropped:

```
dedup product_id | outputlookup meh_products
```

Very simply, this will first deduplicate the results based on `product_id`, since we are only interested in having a single `product_id` listed. Secondly, we output the results of the `stats` command to the `meh_products` lookup, as we have it configured. This writes the data to the disk, which overwrites the existing file in the process, so make sure that your search is correct before executing the search.

 The deduplication may cause you to lose records from your lookup, most notably when the field has a many-to-one relationship!

Now that you have a saved search generating the lookup file, you can use the file! Very simply, execute the following search:

```
|inputlookup meh_products
```
```

Since this is the first command in the search string, it will pull in the content of the CSV into a table. From here, you can modify the data, add more data, or use it in a subsearch. You can even use this lookup to add fields to your existing data. Based on our example data, we have `deal.id` as a field in the raw event. To enrich the raw data, execute a search like this:

```
`meh_base` earliest=-3h@h | lookup meh_products product_id AS deal.id
| ...
```

The `lookup` command is used to pull in lookup data based on existing data in the raw event. First, you specify which lookup you want to use. In this case, we are using `meh_products`. The next part of the command states: look up the data in the file by `product_id`, with the raw field name of `deal.id`. This maps `deal.id` to `product_id` and then looks for the value of `product_id` within the text file. Now, in the field list, there are the `product_date` and `product_title` fields, to name a few. The same thing applies here; you can use these new fields in the rest of the search as any other field. The really magical part with lookups is that these are replicated to the search peers as part of the search bundle. These files don't necessarily need to exist on the search peers. However, be aware that the larger the lookup files, the larger the bundles, and the bundles will need extra time to be transmitted to the search peers. Keep them small, or replicate the lookups to the indexers locally using rsync. This will help keep things smooth and fast.

External lookups are scripts that are executed during the search command execution. Instead of looking for data from a flat file, the external lookup executes a command, or series of commands, and returns the data from that execution. The example we will look at is the DNS lookup provided with Splunk. To configure an external lookup, we need to edit the `transforms.conf` file once again. The Splunk-provided file has this configuration, which can be found at `http://docs.splunk.com/Documentation/Splunk`:

```
[dnslookup]
external_cmd = external_lookup.py clienthost clientip
fields_list = clienthost,clientip
```

The `external_lookup.py` Python script is located at `$SPLUNK_HOME/etc/system/default/bin`. This script connects to a DNS server and performs a lookup based on whether a host name or an IP address was passed to the script. The lookup is called right in a search bar, just like other lookups:

```
index=_internal | head 1 | lookup dnslookup clienthost AS host | ...
```

This search pulls the first event from the internal index, performs a DNS lookup on the host name, and returns the IP address. This can be very useful for determining attacking IPs in a security App, or for looking up a web visitor's country to perform further analytics.

Common Information Model

No discussion on data enrichment is complete without at least mentioning the Common Information Model. The CIM within Splunk helps define a least common denominator when it comes to your data. It allows you to normalize your data and use a common set of fields across all data of the same type. For example, in your environment, let's assume that you have an IIS web server and an Apache web server. You are indexing the access logs from each server using the `iis` and `access_combined` source types respectively. The `iis` defines a cookie field as `cs_Cookie`, whereas `access_combined` uses the `cookie` field. Without the CIM, when you do a search for a dashboard or a view, or do just ad hoc searching, you might specify this: `sourcetype=iis OR sourcetype=access_combined | rename cs_Cookie AS cookie | stats count by cookie`. This might seem simple for two source types, but it doesn't scale to, say, 50 different types of web server logs. This is where the CIM is extremely valuable. By field aliasing the `cs_Cookie` field to cookie, you will have two different fields show up, but both will contain the cookie data. The advantage here is that by using the common field, you can quickly bring a new source type online, without having to edit your searches and dashboards. In this case, you might also tag source types to get `web_log` or something descriptive that will help identify the different source types. Now, with tagging and CIM, your search will be more like this: `tag=web_log | stats count by cookie` — much simpler to read, and it scales effectively. Splunk provides a CIM App (`https://apps.splunk.com/app/1621/`) that contains data models for 21 different domains of data. A domain of data is simply a category that reaches a subset of data. For example, you may have a certificates domain, or perhaps an e-mail domain. For the most up-to-date information on the CIM, refer to the Splunk documentation at `http://docs.splunk.com/Documentation/CIM/latest/User/Overview`. Planning your inputs and applying CIM from the beginning will help you scale and search effectively after the initial consumption of data. The CIM is based more on concepts and abstraction of data, and while it shines in theory, the practical implementation and debugging can be time consuming. Start small and work your way up, one source type at a time.

Branding your App

Branding your App allows end users to know who you are and provides them with a consistent representation of your brand. Splunk offers almost limitless options for customization and brand creation within a Splunk App. SimpleXML provides a small subset of customization, and if you employ the full **Splunk Developer's Kit (SDK)**, you will get limitless control over presentation and branding. There are a few guidelines for rebranding your App, and the most up-to-date information can be found at `http://www.splunk.com/view/SP-CAAAFT9`.

The guidelines are as follows:

- Keeping the Splunk logo in place and adding their text to the right of it, for example, *Splunk> Foo* where their add-on is named *Foo*. This is the recommended action when Splunk's visual elements are left mostly intact.

- Replacing the Splunk logo with the developer's logo and then slotting in the *Splunk-Powered* logo to the right. This is the recommended action when the developer creates a branded UI with a different look and feel from the usual visual experience of Splunk. The *Splunk-Powered* logo must remain in its original state, including size and color.

- When exporting Splunk's visual elements, such as a chart, graph, map, or other data visualization to another web page, App, or platform, the *Splunk-Powered* logo must be visible somewhere within the page that displays the Splunk visual element. Because of space consideration, the logo need not be original size, but must remain the same color and be legible to the human eye.

 These are the official guidelines from Splunk and are subject to change at any time. We recommend referring to Splunk's website, at `http://www.splunk.com/`, for the latest and most up-to-date information.

Logos

Logos are a visual representation of your App. A well-thought-out and well-executed icon and logo can help your App be quickly identified from a larger list of Apps, specifically on Splunkbase. Most companies and organizations, and some individuals, have their own icon. Apps definitely support icons and display them in a few different areas. App icons are stored in a special folder named `static` within the App. There are requirements for each size of an icon and logo, as shown in the following table. This table can be found at `http://docs.splunk.com/Documentation/Splunk/6.2.1/AdvancedDev/AddConfigurations`.

Filename	Total image size*	Suggested use area	Placement**
`appIcon.png`	36 x 36	36 x 36 or less. If the box is totally filled, it may feel too big.	App list on the Splunk home page (standard-resolution displays)

Filename	Total image size*	Suggested use area	Placement**
appIcon_2x.png	72 x 72	72 x 72 or less.	App list on the Splunk home page (high-resolution displays)
appIconAlt.png	36 x 36	36 x 36 or less.	App menus for Splunk Bar and Search Bar (standard-resolution displays)
appIconAlt_2x.png	72 x 72	72 x 72 or less.	App menus for Splunk Bar and Search Bar (high-resolution displays)
appLogo.png	160 x 40 (maximum size)	160 x 40 (maximum size; leave some vertical margin).	App Bar on standard resolution displays
appLogo_2x.png	320 x 80 (maximum size)	320 x 80 (maximum size; leave some vertical margin).	App Bar on high-resolution displays

*The image sizes are in pixels

**High-resolution displays include MacBook Pro with retina display

So now that you know the requirements, let's create an icon and logo for our *Splunk Developer's Guide* App. Very simply, we want to use a gear icon. This was found via Google Image search and is free for use anywhere. The important part to note is that it is an SVG image. This allows us to create PNG graphics that scale correctly. Here, we will use the GIMP photo editing software, as it is free for anybody to use. In order to create the icon, we open the SVG in GIMP, which asks us to scale the image. We started with 36 x 36 pixels and then created the 72 x 72 pixel image.

Both of these are placed in the `static` folder within the root of the App, or in other words, `$APP_HOME/static`. We copied them both again and renamed them to fit the `appIconAlt.png` images, so either way, our images are the same. To create the logos, we opened the gear in the correct height and then resized the image to get the correct width. We added some text and exported the images to a PNG file. The final logo outcomes are as follows; notice how well they scaled:

You don't always have to use SVG, but it will definitely help when resizing to match the size requirements. The images have had a border placed around them to show the actual size, and although you can't see it, they actually have transparent backgrounds so that our navigation bar can contain a color without having to change the icons. Once you have placed your App icon and logo images in the `static` folder, they will appear in the Splunk interface. The logo is situated in the top-right corner of the page, underneath the web interface menus. The App icon shows up in the App menu on the left-hand side of the screen, as well as on the left-hand side of the launcher App:

Using an icon and logo is a quick way to personalize your App and make it easily recognizable to end users and new users alike.

Navigation

Navigation is paramount in directing your end users to the different dashboards in your App. Splunk comes with default navigation, but you will most likely want to customize it for your App. This will help remove unnecessary views, dashboards, and reports from your App, and include only those things relevant to your App and in the structure you define. Let's build a SimpleXML file for your first bit of navigation. Since we don't have any views or dashboards yet, it will be really simple. We will simply link to the default *search* view and modify the color of the navigation bar. The file for this is located in `$APP_HOME/default/data/ui/nav/` and is titled `default.xml`. Therefore, the full path to edit will be `$APP_HOME/default/data/ui/nav/default.xml`. Edit this file by adding these lines to it:

```
<nav search_view="search" color="#355e3b">
  <view name="search" default="true" label="Search"/>
  <view name="pivot" />
  <view name="reports" />
  <view name="alerts" />
  <view name="dashboards" />
</nav>
```

Let's break it down. Firstly, we start with the special `nav` xml tag. The `search_view` and `color` attributes control the default search view to use and the color of the navigation bar respectively. In this App, our search bar will be hunter green, which is `#355E3B` in hex. Once you have those attributes filled in, you can start adding content into the navigation bar. Each item becomes nested underneath the other items in the typical XML fashion. Since we currently need only the search bar to be shown, we enter a `view` tag, with some attributes.

The `name` attribute refers to the name of the view to use, not what will be shown on the page; that is the `label` attribute's job. The `default` attribute sets this view item as the first to be shown when an end user enters the App. The resulting rendering of the navigation bar looks pretty nice. Do you see where the logo shows up?

This is the most basic navigation menu you can create. You can also create and edit this navigation configuration via the web interface. Simply navigate to **Settings** | **User Interface** | **Navigation menus** and edit the default configuration. You will still have to enter the XML by hand; there isn't a prebuilt manager here to take care of it for you. Let's leave the navigation alone for now. Once we have some dashboards and views, we will add them at that time.

 If you define a view within your navigation XML but that view doesn't exist within Splunk, that section of the menu will not show up in the navigation bar.

CSS

Cascading Style Sheets (CSS) have become an integral part of HTML and web presentations. Splunk takes advantage of this, and by providing your own CSS, you can rebrand a large chunk of the web interface. HTML and SimpleXML views are different in the ways in which the CSS is called. Your CSS files for the App need to be stored within the App, notably in `$APP_HOME/appserver/static`. These files are then called from the SimpleXML and HTML dashboards and included in the rendered pages. We will cover this in more depth when we begin building our views and dashboards.

JavaScript

JavaScript is an integral part of the Splunk web interface. Even SimpleXML is controlled (behind the scenes) by JavaScript frameworks. This flexibility gives you many options for customizing the interface, and much like the custom CSS, the custom JS is stored under `$APP_HOME/appserver/static`. You can use subfolders to keep things organized, but the basic `dashboard.js` file should be kept under the base folder. We will dive head first into some custom JavaScript in a moment.

 The default search view does not load custom JavaScript or CSS. Therefore, it cannot have customized CSS or JavaScript. You will have to build your own view for customizing.

Acceleration

Splunk searches are fast. They can pull millions of events in a relatively small amount of time. However, what happens when you need to search billions of events? Also, what if you want the daily statistics of a website over 5 years? This is where some methods of acceleration will give you an advantage over raw data. Acceleration *summarizes* your data and provides you with aggregated statistics that can be looked up faster. If your App doesn't collect that much data, or you don't care about long-term statistics, you might not need any form of acceleration.

Summary indexing

Summary indexing is a tested but true method of collecting aggregated data. One way is to set up the summary fields and place them in the index using the `collect` command.

Summary indexing does not count towards your daily license usage, so feel free to summarize as much data as you wish!

Let's start with the report manager. Before we begin configuring the summary index, we have to decide what we want to summarize. Looking at the sample data at the end of this chapter, we can see that meh has included information regarding their daily poll. Our script polls the API every 5 minutes, which gives us 288 events per day. Over a span of a year, that's a total of 105,120 different events with poll data. This is still not a huge amount for Splunk to handle, but for the sake of argument, let's say we want to speed up the reports that are using this data. By summarizing the poll data every hour, we will have 24 events per day, or 8,760 events per year. This is a significant reduction in the number of events we need to search for, and since they will be collected within a specific summary index, we will also optimize the search at the same time. In dealing with the poll data, we created a macro to correlate the answers to their values. We call it `pollExtraction` and use it in the summary creation search.

To create the summary search, we start with the base search for gathering poll data:

```
'meh_base' earliest=-1h@h latest=@h |'pollExtraction' | stats
max(votes) as votes latest(timestamp) as PollDate latest(PollId) as
PollId by answer PollTitle | collect index=summary
```

Let's break it down. We've seen `meh_base` before; it pulls data from the scripted input. Since we want to summarize the previous hour, we will restrict the time range and run the search at 1 minute past the hour. The `pollExtraction` macro performs various `mvzip` and `mvexpand` commands that correlate the data correctly. Next, we perform a statistic report and pull the maximum number of votes by each answer. Since our data increases over time, we only need the highest number of votes per hour. We add the `PollTitle`, `PollId`, and `PollDate` attributes to the `by` clause so that when we load the report later, we will have the data we need to display it properly. The final command, `collect`, takes the results from the statistic report and puts the event into the index defined in the command, `summary` in this case. Now that we have created the search, we can save it and schedule it to run at 15 minutes past the hour. Here is a sample of what the resulting summary event looks like:

```
01/30/2015 21:00:00 -0500, info_min_time=1422669600.000, info_max_
time=1422673200.000, info_search_time=1422676498.182, PollDate="Fri,
30 Jan 2015 21:59:39 EST", PollId=a6li0000000PCCCAA4,
PollTitle="Who's going to win the Super Bowl?", answer="Some other
team you'll bet on in the forum!", votes=23
```

To pull the summary events in a search, you can target the index and the other fields in the event to get the correct data:

```
index=summary earliest=-2h@h PollTitle=*
```

This will pull only as many events as there are in the last 2 hours in the index summary. This speeds up the creation of dashboards and other reports based on the aggregated data. If the need arises, you can also add markers to the data. For example, if you add | `eval marker=meh_poll` to the summary-generating search before the `collect` command, you can then search for your data like this:

```
index=summary earliest=-2h@h marker=meh_poll
```

This methodology will work for any type of statistic aggregation of values, including averages, minimums, maximums, and other functions supported by the `statistic` command. This style of summary indexing is decidedly *old school* in its approach and doesn't take advantage of any of the newer `si-` commands.

Accelerated reports

Splunk 6 offers a new kind of acceleration. This type of acceleration applies to saved reports (previously known as saved searches). It can only be used on *transforming searches*, or searches that use transforming commands within them. Additionally, if there are any other commands prior to the transforming command, they must also be streaming commands. Transforming commands are those similar to `timechart`, `stats`, `chart`, or `top`. Streaming commands are those similar to `where`, `eval`, `regex`, `bin`, or any others that can run on the indexer. This is an important note to make, as when approaching summary indexing the *old school* way, you can use any command to generate the table of results that is placed in the summary index. Report acceleration is different. Report acceleration stores the summarizations parallel to the buckets that hold the raw data. Splunk will also automatically regenerate any missing summaries, which is something an administrator would have to do using the *old school* method. Another caveat of the accelerated report is that the summaries are not replicated within a cluster, so if an indexer in a cluster goes offline, the summaries that were housed in those buckets need to be regenerated, which draws a load off of the remaining indexers. Report acceleration can be very useful over large datasets, and requires very little human interaction to get them working. Simply create a qualifying search and enable acceleration, and off Splunk goes to provide you with those summaries. The full documentation for report acceleration is very in-depth and can be found at `http://docs.splunk.com/Documentation/Splunk/latest/Knowledge/Manageacceleratedsearchsummaries`.

Summary

In this chapter, we went through various methods of enriching data. By adding more tags, event types, and workflow actions to your App, you can provide various enhancements for your end users, creating a unified and seamless environment. We showed you how using lookups provides a means of enhancing data, and how you can start branding your App according to your specifications. We will elaborate on these customizations as we move forward. We also looked at some methods of accelerating data and provided an example of how to do so.

In the next chapter, we will start covering the use and configuration of SimpleXML views and dashboards. We won't delve extensively into SimpleXML, but will cover some basic visualizations and how to create and use a SimpleXML form.

4

Basic Views and Dashboards

In this chapter, we will use a web interface to start creating basic views and dashboards that will help visualize the data we have been collecting and enhancing. Knowing what data you have and how it is arranged is paramount for quickly building views and dashboards. It also gives you a place to start, and shows which parts of your data get displayed on which dashboard. Yeah, you can go ahead and just start creating dashboards, views, and saved searches, but with a little bit of planning, you can avoid refactoring multiple times. As with any project, setting the scope of what your App is going to address is a key factor in its making. After we tackle the broad questions on what to include and how, we will cover the following topics: using a saved search in a panel and the different types of visualizations available by default in Splunk. We will use some of these saved searches and visualizations to create a SimpleXML dashboard, and then convert that dashboard into a SimpleXML form. We will also briefly discuss HTML dashboards, but those will be covered in depth in the next chapter. Therefore, we will only show you how to convert existing dashboards and create new ones from scratch.

Knowing your data

Knowing your data is paramount when creating dashboards and views. Being familiar with your data gives you a deeper understanding of the context and a greater insight into the different nuances of data visualization. For example, you will never use time series data in a pie chart, right? Knowing that you have time series data before trying to create a chart will speed up the process of designing and creating the dashboards you will need in your App. Another very valid thought process entails you to think about which data fits which data visualization; it's more than just the typical pie versus time-based line charts. This can include such things as choosing between bar and column charts, when to use stacked bars, or whether you should use 100 percent stacked bars. Some of these will be answered only once you work with the visualization previews available in Splunk.

Let's start with a quick exercise. Let's assume that you are collecting Kbps metrics for your Internet connection. You collect these metrics every five minutes and index them in Splunk. What kind of graph would best leverage time-based statistics? A line graph? Area graphs? Yes! Bar graphs? Pie graphs? No! Bar and pie graphs do not adequately show time-based data. However, on the other hand, if you were trying to determine the percentage of users using the Internet who were in specific ranges of age, should you use a line graph? Probably not, as this type of data will fit better within a pie graph or bar graph. This is because you are interested in statistics over all your time range, not just in specific time intervals (such as five minutes).

Available modules

Let's get a quick overview of the types of charts available in Splunk 6.2 and beyond. These are charts that can be used directly from the dashboard editor. The built-in visualizations are as follows: **Line**, **Area**, **Column**, **Bar**, **Pie**, **Scatter**, **Bubble**, **Single Value**, **Radial Gauge**, **Filler Gauge**, **Marker Gauge**, and **Map**. Each of these displays data differently, and, obviously, not all data will fit into all types of visualizations. Splunk helps you know your data and offers recommendations based on the search you have completed, as shown in the following screenshot. The example search used a `timechart` command, so the recommended charts were those that deal well with time-based data—**Line**, **Area**, and **Column**:

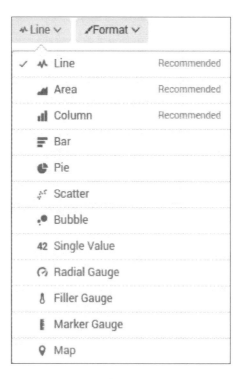

As you can see, these are the native charts in Splunk. Additional modules are available or can be created, but these are the basic visualizations.

SimpleXML dashboard

Okay, so now we get to play around with some visualizations. Let's create a dashboard with some visualizations of our data from `https://meh.com/`. For now, we will limit ourselves to the native visualizations. We will start with the `meh_products` lookup that we have generated. Each product is listed as either **New** or **Refurbished**, so let's see how that makes a chart:

```
| inputlookup meh_products | top product_condition
```

This will be our basic search that pulls the `meh_products` lookup, which is kept populated by the saved search we had written earlier. We are only interested in knowing the distribution of product conditions over the entire time range, so we will choose a pie chart from the drop-down menu. This gives us a pie chart like this one:

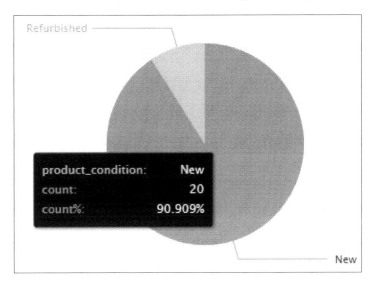

As you can see, at the time of writing this book, and with the amount of data collected, the top condition at **90.909%** is New. Now, let's save this as a panel in a new dashboard. We will call the dashboard **Overview**. We do this by clicking on the **Save As** drop-down menu in the top-right corner of the screen. You would want to save it as **Dashboard Panel**. This pops up a dialog to create a new dashboard, or append this visualization to an existing dashboard. We want to create a new dashboard. Fill in the form, as shown in the following screenshot, and then click on **Save**.

Since we are developing a full-blown App, we want to make sure that this dashboard is created in the App, and not in our user folder. So, make sure that the **Shared in App** option is selected:

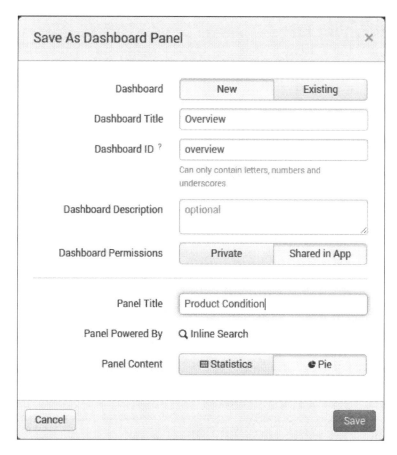

This will create the dashboard and place that pie chart on it. Once you have this created, you need a way to quickly get to the dashboard. Let's edit the `default.xml` file (located in `default/data/ui/nav`) and add the name of this dashboard. Add the following line to the XML file, right under the `nav` tag of the file. Hit the debug/ refresh endpoint to load the change:

```
<view name="overview" default="true" />
```

When you navigate to the app, this **Overview** dashboard will be the first to load. Let's add some more data visualizations, shall we? You can add as many as you want, but keep in mind that if more visualizations are added, more searches will need to be dispatched, and this may decrease search performance of the search head.

This is what we came up with; isn't it pretty?

All these data points are calculated from the `meh_products` lookup file, and they cover all the items located therein. However, what if we want time-based data? Let's create another dashboard. This one will use the summaries of the `https://meh.com/` polls that we have been collecting. We won't go step by step as we create the time poll data dashboard; the steps are fairly similar to before. Don't forget to add your new dashboard to the navigation! The following screenshot gives us the poll results:

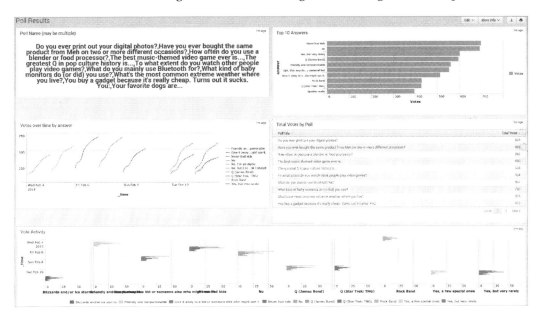

Wow! That was quick. Do you see how we are using line charts and bar charts to display time-based data? But wait! The data looks funny. That is because this dashboard is showing everything over all the time for which we collected data. A new poll starts every day, with new answers, so this dashboard currently shows the aggregate of the entire collection. Not really useful in the grand scheme of things, which leads us to… SimpleXML forms!

SimpleXML forms

A SimpleXML form allows you to convert a SimpleXML dashboard into a dashboard with inputs. This allows you to narrow down the set of information from all time to a defined range of time. Let's go ahead and convert this dashboard into a form. Find the **Edit** drop-down menu in the top-right corner of the dashboard, and then choose **Edit Panels**. Here, you will see **Add Input**. Click on this and select **Time**. There are also other options available, as you can see in this screenshot:

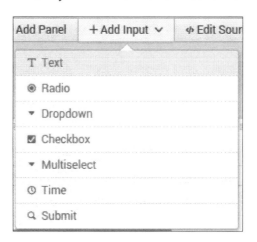

Clicking on **Time** will add a drop-down in the top-left corner of the dashboard. Now, it is considered a form. While still in edit mode, select the time range picker and set the value to **Today**. This will load only today's data into the form that was created. To leverage this new restriction, you must update each panel. Edit each panel search, click on the **Edit Search String** item and update **Time Range Scope** to **Shared Time Picker (field1)**. This will allow each panel to use the time range picked in the drop-down at the top of the form. Once you have edited all the panels, click on the **Done** button in the top-right corner, and then refresh the page. You will notice that the data is cleaner and displays only a single poll's information. This allows the information to be displayed cleanly and with context. Remember that chart from the bottom of the dashboard? Ugly, wasn't it? Very cluttered and not useful; now that same chart is nicely clean and displays data in two dimensions.

The data here uses a bar chart, with each answer as a different color (and column). This chart gives you a time-based representation of poll results. Time is shown from top (midnight) to bottom. Each different color represents a different poll response, and from left to right is the calculated difference in the number of votes (essentially, it is the distance from one data point to the next in the summary), which shows the number of additional votes that that answer received from the previous time frame in the summary:

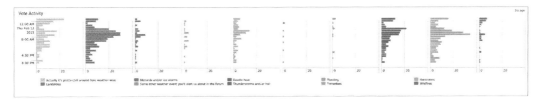

Let's look a little closer at a few bars. The following screenshot shows a close-up of the far left answer. As you can see, there is a lot of activity in the first few hours of the day, and it steadily decreases over the course of the day:

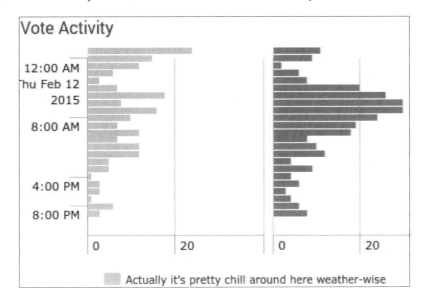

While this might not be a common use for bar charts, it represents the data differently, while giving context to each data point.

Now that we have the form responding to a specific time range, let's clean up the search activity. As it currently stands, each panel in this form executes a new search. That's not very effective, especially when the dataset could be massive. So, let's talk about post-processing. What is post-processing? Essentially, we will define a single search element for the dashboard. Then, we will use those search results in every other panel of the dashboard — one base search transformed and processed multiple times. We start by editing the source of the form, located under the **Edit** drop-down (find the **Edit Source** option). Now, add in this XML code, right before the first `<row>` tag:

```
<search id="baseSearch">
    <query>
      index=summary category=meh_poll | bucket span=1h _time | stats
count avg(votes) as votes by _time PollTitle answer | fields - count
    </query>
    <earliest>$field1.earliest$</earliest>
    <latest>$field1.latest$</latest>
</search>
```

This sets up the base search for all other panels that reference the `baseSearch` ID. Did you notice the `$field1.earliest$` token? It refers to the time picker drop-down that was added earlier in the section where we converted this dashboard into a form. Don't worry about it for now; just add it in there, as shown. Now find your first panel. You will see a `<search>` tag underneath the `<title>` tag.

Add `base="baseSearch"` to the `<search>` tag and change the `<query>` tag to have only the `stats` command. You should end up with something like this:

```
<search base="baseSearch">
        <query>stats values(PollTitle)</query>
</search>
```

Do this for each panel in the form. Once you're done, click on the **Save** button. Now each panel within your form will load as soon as the main search is done. In this way, you can speed up the rendering of the form without extolling a huge search cost on your infrastructure.

Post-processing should only be used on data that has been transformed in some way. It is not a best practice to use raw events, mainly due to the 500,000 event limitation and restriction of the post processing module. There is also a timeout in Splunk Web that may be reached if you are searching for large datasets. In our example, we used the `stats` command to transform the data into a table with only a selected number of fields and already calculated hourly votes. This helps to optimize the base search and prevents us from reaching the limit.

Another great optimization trick is to use a scheduled search, summary index, or data model as the base search.

Warning

Dashboards with an excessive number of searches can cause the search performance to degrade, causing issues within a production environment. Use optimization tricks and configurations to keep the searches running clean.

Let's circle back to that `$field1.earliest$` item we saw earlier. This is a tokenized field. Splunk tokenizes the variable, allowing dynamic drill-downs and conditional displays and capturing inputs. You can then reference the *tokenized* element using the `$variable$` name. We are going to implement one of these to dynamically limit the results shown, based on the number of votes for an answer. Firstly, click on the **Add Input** button (after entering edit mode, of course), and add a **Text** box. Once it is placed in the field set in the top-left corner, click on the little pencil icon to edit the field. Enter the values shown in this screenshot:

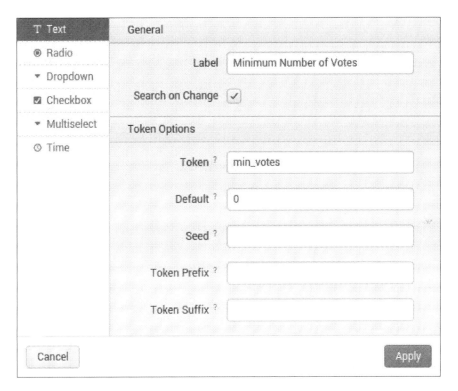

Click on the **Apply** button and then on the **Done** button to finish creating the panel. Now, you would want to add that limitation to your searches, so pick a search that you want to restrict. Add the token name (surrounded by $) to the search as if you were specifying a field. For example, we might only want the answers with more than 100 votes to be displayed on our time-based line chart. The original post process query is this:

```
where isint(votes) | timechart span=1h max(votes) as Votes by
answer useother=f
```

We will update it to the following:

```
where isint(votes) AND votes > $min_votes$| timechart span=1h
max(votes) as Votes by answer useother=f | eval threshold =
$min_votes$.
```

Save the panel and refresh the form. The default value is 0, which is meant to include all results, but once it is changed to 100, the chart displays only the answers that have more than 100 votes, in effect, showing when each answer crossed the threshold:

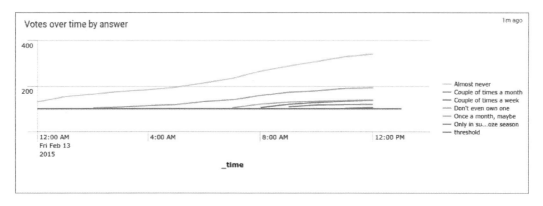

Custom JavaScript, CSS, and Tokens

There will be times when you will want to integrate custom visualizations, custom CSS, or helper JavaScript into a SimpleXML dashboard. Thankfully, we have been provided a way to do so. At the very top of the dashboard/form source code, you will either see the `<dashboard>` or `<form>` tag. Within those tags, as attributes, is where you will declare what scripts should be included in your dashboard:

```
<dashboard script="my_script.js" stylesheet="my_style.css">
```

This allows the loading of custom scripts and CSS from the `$APP_HOME/appserver/static` folder. Placing these files into that folder gives the dashboard access to them. From here, you can interact with the dashboard using jQuery, or another framework, and make it bend to your will.

Another feature of SimpleXML is the ability to manipulate tokens. Let's take, for example, the text input. Let's define it like this in the source code:

```
<input type="text" token="foo">
  <label>Input</label>
  <change>
    <set token="my_new_token">"$value$, Rose!"</set>
  </change>
</input>
```

What does this do? Firstly, it is a text input, so the user will just place whatever they are searching for within that input, and then when it changes, it will update the `my_new_token` token to have a new value. For example, if the user places `fantastic` into the input box, the resulting value of the `my_new_token` token will be `fantastic, Rose!` This is a very simple modification of a token; there are other methods and conditions that can be set on different tags within the SimpleXML. You can find them very nicely documented at `http://docs.splunk.com/Documentation/Splunk/latest/Viz/tokens`.

There are many, many other options available for SimpleXML forms and dashboards. Since the use cases far outweigh the space required to detail them, we'll let you discover and explore the specifications for SimpleXML yourself, and instead turn towards HTML dashboards.

HTML dashboards

HTML dashboards are simply that. These are dashboards that have been either written from scratch in HTML and JavaScript, or converted from a SimpleXML dashboard. The primary purpose of an HTML dashboard is to give the developer the greatest degree of freedom possible. Anything that you can do in HTML with CSS and JavaScript can most likely be done in an HTML dashboard as well, with the added benefit of being able to use the entirety of Splunk information.

Let's go ahead and convert a SimpleXML dashboard into an HTML dashboard. Let's use the Overview dashboard we created earlier. To convert an existing dashboard, simply navigate to it in the web UI, then click on the **Edit** dropdown, and then click on **Convert to HTML**. A dialog will show up, and you will want to click on **Replace Current** in this instance. If you're creating HTML dashboards for the first time, you may want to use **Create New** until you feel comfortable with the process:

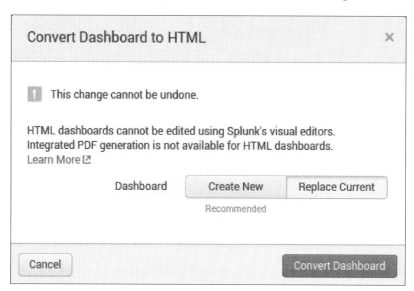

Convert Dashboard to HTML ✕

This change cannot be undone.

HTML dashboards cannot be edited using Splunk's visual editors. Integrated PDF generation is not available for HTML dashboards. Learn More ⎘

Dashboard   Create New   Replace Current

Recommended

Cancel   Convert Dashboard

Warning

Replacing a dashboard is *permanent*; there is no undo feature. You will also lose the ability to edit the panels directly in the editor, and you will not be able to generate a PDF file from the dashboard.

If you are ready, click on **Convert Dashboard**. You can then click on **View** to view the dashboard. What has changed? Nothing visually, really. The real magic happens behind the scenes, and we will delve into this in the next chapter. However, say you wanted to create a new HTML dashboard from scratch. The easiest way is to create a blank SimpleXML dashboard and then convert it inline. This will prepopulate all of the HTML and JavaScript you will need to get started with building a dashboard from scratch.

Summary

In this chapter, we covered some basic aspects of dashboards and view creation. Making sure you know your data is paramount for successful execution in data visualization. Splunk helps you discover your data, but you need to understand your data to display it properly. Not all data types and results fit into all chart types.

We also covered creating a SimpleXML dashboard and then converting that dashboard into a form. SimpleXML dashboards give you ease of creation and allow you to manipulate them within the web interface. This is an excellent option for quick displays of data, without diving too deep into the code. We also briefly introduced HTML dashboards. There are several advantages of HTML dashboards, especially the added benefits of using the entire HTML, CSS, and JavaScript stacks.

In our next chapter, we will start the joys of HTML dashboarding and see how to use the SplunkJS Stack effectively.

5
The Splunk Web Framework

In this chapter, we will dive directly into HTML dashboards and the Splunk Web Framework. This won't be just an overview, this is some serious coding. This is the nuts and bolts for all the newer apps being written and produced, as it provides the best options for customization and visualization. There is a basic structure, and some rather important points that need to be made, and some additional information on how to brand using custom CSS and JavaScript. We will explore the SplunkJS stack, and go over how the objects are used in their native form, and show how you can customize them. We will add a custom visualization using a D3 chart and place it in the dashboard. Using D3 charts allows for so much additional extensibility and presentation. We will also cover adding external data sources (via REST APIs and other methods) using the jQuery library.

The HTML dashboard

The HTML dashboard can either be generated from an existing SimpleXML dashboard, or it can be written by hand. We recommend creating a SimpleXML dashboard and then converting it. This ensures that the most up-to-date code is generated from the version you are using. For a refresher on how to convert a SimpleXML dashboard to an HTML dashboard, see *Chapter 4*, *Basic Views and Dashboards*. The Splunk Web Framework is built into the HTML dashboard and into the core programming of Splunk. The framework is designed to allow maximum extensibility and versatility in the development of dashboards.

The basic code of the previously generated dashboard (see *Chapter 4*, *Basic Views and Dashboards* — the dashboard is called *Overview*) contains various items that are consistent across dashboards. Generally, all of the HTML and CSS definitions are placed within the dashboard code first, with the JavaScript portion at the end. This is a pretty standard best practice, as this allows the page to load most of the way through without hitting a loading problem because of the data.

The first important bit of the HTML dashboard is the inclusion of the Bootstrap CSS, as shown in the following code:

```
<link rel="stylesheet" type="text/css"
href="/en-US/static/@237341/css/build/bootstrap.min.css" />
<link rel="stylesheet" type="text/css"
href="/en-US/static/@237341/css/build/pages/dashboard-simple-
bootstrap.min.css" />
```

Bootstrap (`http://getbootstrap.com/`) is a popular framework aimed at helping designers create robust and responsive web pages and projects. We won't dive into Bootstrap too much, but it is important when working with the default grid patterns in the dashboard. The first line includes the base Bootstrap CSS file. The second line includes the Splunk-specific Bootstrap CSS file. These configurations give Splunk its native branding and presentation. Let's dissect `href` for the `include` file:

- `/en-US`: This is the locale for your installation. By default, it is en-US, but can be configured to be different.

- `/static`: This indicates that the files are static and are cached appropriately.

- `/@237341`: This is your Splunk-specific build number. This number is updated every time you upgrade core Splunk. The idea behind changing the number in `include href` is simple: it breaks the cache on that object during core Splunk upgrades.

- `/css/build/pages/`: This is the path to the CSS files for pages.

- `dashboard-simple-bootstrap.min.css`: This is the filename that contains the Splunk-native CSS.

 If you need to bust the cache to load new files from disk, you can use the *bump* URL. Navigate to `http://<your host and port>/en-US/_bump` and click on the **Bump Version** button. This will update your version number by 1, so the version number may look like `@237341.2` and increment from there with each click.

You will find this convention multiple times throughout the dashboard. You will have the ability to include custom CSS files, but let's look at the next important part of the dashboard, the navigation.

As you can see from the code in the next code block, the page is designed to be compliant to section 508. If you aren't familiar with it, section 508 refers to the laws and regulations that web pages should comply with that allow universal accessibility. Using a typical browser, the first `<a>` tag won't appear; it only appears if the user is using a screen reader. Following this tag, the next `<div>` tag gives a place for the Splunk header to be placed. This header includes the administrative navigation **Settings**, **Messages**, **Activity**, and more such options as well as the application navigation. Notice the special code piece located in the `placeholder-Splunk-bar` div tag. The `{{SPLUNKWEB_URL_PREFIX}}` is a placeholder for the user's locale information and is generated on the fly when rendered in the browser. The generated HTML is shown here:

```
<a class="navSkip" href="#navSkip" tabindex="1">Screen reader
users, click here to skip the navigation bar</a>
<div class="header splunk-header">
    <div id="placeholder-splunk-bar">
        <a href="{{SPLUNKWEB_URL_PREFIX}}/app/launcher/home"
class="brand" title="splunk &gt; listen to your
data">splunk<strong>&gt;</strong></a>
    </div>
    <div id="placeholder-app-bar"></div>
</div>
<a id="navSkip"></a>
```

This HTML, when rendered, appears as shown in the following screenshot:

This piece is important because without it, the navigation bars would not work correctly. As we progress further, you will see where the SplunkJS stack makes its mark on the dashboard and navigation. Next up in the progression down the page, we enter the actual HTML layout of the panels. These panels are the generated code from the SimpleXML that we converted earlier, as you can see in the following result:

```
<div id="row1" class="dashboard-row dashboard-row1">
    <div id="panel1" class="dashboard-cell" style="width: 20%;">
        <div class="dashboard-panel clearfix">
            <div class="panel-element-row">
            <div id="element1" class="dashboard-element single"
style="width: 100%">
                <div class="panel-head">
                  <h3>Total Revenue</h3>
                </div>
                <div class="panel-body"></div>
```

```
        </div>
      </div>
    </div>
  </div>
```

This HTML, when rendered, appears as shown in the following panel:

There are currently seven panels on the **overview** page, each one using similar HTML. All of the CSS for these panels can be overridden using custom CSS files, along with most other styling on the page.

As we progress even further into the rabbit hole, we are now at the JavaScript portion of the page. Splunk uses the RequireJS framework to include many different modules to be used on the page. Each different visualization has its own `require` module and needs to be included if it is going to be used on the page. Let's start with the basic configuration statement:

```
require.config({
    baseUrl: "{{SPLUNKWEB_URL_PREFIX}}/static/js",
    waitSeconds: 0 // Disable require.js load timeout
});
```

This is the configuration for the RequireJS framework. The `baseUrl` variable points to the static JavaScript location for the native Splunk libraries. Later on, we will use a modified `require` configuration to include custom modules and help resolve dependencies. When you convert a SimpleXML dashboard into an HTML dashboard, Splunk very helpfully includes comments in the JavaScript code to guide you into the proper configuration of the RequireJS framework. The next part of the code requires the libraries that are needed to load the page:

```
require([
    "splunkjs/mvc",
    "splunkjs/mvc/utils",
    ...
    ],
```

```
function(
    mvc,
    utils,
    ...
) { ...
```

Each item in this `require` statement is appended to `baseUrl` in the configuration. The JavaScript file is then included and placed into the variable located in the following function. So the `{{SPLUNKWEB_URL_PREFIX}}/static/js/splunkjs/mvc.js` file is then stored in the `mvc` variable. These variables are then used within the `main` function to perform the actual tasks needed to collect and display the data.

 Due to the complex nature of the HTML dashboard, it is recommend that you create a blank SimpleXML dashboard, and then convert it, before building out the searches and visualizations. This ensures that you have all the basic libraries you need, cutting down on development time.

Following the `require` statement, and the start of the function, we can now move into defining what the SplunkJS stack interacts with on the page and how it creates the different elements.

SplunkJS Stack

SplunkJS Stack contains a few frameworks to help web developers build Splunk applications in a familiar JavaScript environment. The first is Backbone.js, which provides the MVC framework as building blocks for your dashboards. The second is RequireJS, which helps to manage dependencies. The third is jQuery, which helps to manage the document objects within the dashboard. Finally, Splunk provides a large library with views and managers that help you interact with Splunk. We would be remiss if we didn't take some time and review the different views and managers. Each of these is implemented within the JavaScript code of the RequireJS function.

As we start looking into each item of the Splunk library, we will present the native module path and the default variable name. These get placed in the RequireJS function call as noted earlier. This can be abstracted in the following manner:

```
require([ "<splunk module path>" ],
    function( <splunk variable name> ) {
    var example_1 = new <splunk variable name> ({
<options> });
    });
```

After the defaults are given, a sample instantiation will be displayed, with some basic options. These options will be explained at a higher level, and a link to the documentation will give you the detailed view of each option.

Search-related modules

Let's talk JavaScript modules. For each module, we will review their primary purpose, their module path, the default variable used in an HTML dashboard, and the JavaScript instantiation of the module. We will also cover which attributes are required and which are optional.

SearchManager

The **SearchManager** is a primary driver of any dashboard. This module contains an entire search job, including the query, properties, and the actual dispatch of the job. Let's instantiate an object and dissect the options from this sample code:

```
Module Path: splunkjs/mvc/searchmanager
Default Variable: SearchManager
JavaScript Object instantiation
    Var mySearchManager = new SearchManager({
        id: "search1",
        earliest_time: "-24h@h",
        latest_time: "now",
        preview: true,
        cache: false,
        search: "index=_internal | stats count by sourcetype"
    }, {tokens: true, tokenNamespace: "submitted"});
```

The only required property is the `id` property. This is a reference ID that will be used to access this object from other instantiated objects later in the development of the page. It is best to name it something concise yet descriptive with no spaces. The `search` property is optional and contains the SPL query that will be dispatched from the module. Make sure to escape any quotes properly, if not, you may cause a JavaScript exception. The `earliest_time` and `latest_time` are time modifiers that restrict the range of the events. At the end of the options object, notice the second object with token references. This is what automatically executes the search. Without these options, you would have to trigger the search manually. There are a few other properties shown, but you can refer to the actual documentation at the main documentation page at `http://docs.splunk.com/DocumentationStatic/WebFramework/1.1/compref_searchmanager.html`.

> SearchManagers are set to autostart on page load. To prevent this, set autostart to false in the options.

SavedSearchManager

The **SavedSearchManager** is very similar in operation to the SearchManager, but it works with a saved report, instead of an ad hoc query. The advantage to using a SavedSearchManager is in performance. If the report is scheduled, you can configure the SavedSearchManager to use the previously run jobs to load the data. If any other user runs the report within Splunk, the SavedSearchManager can reuse that user's results in the manager to boost performance. Let's take a look at a few sections of our code:

```
Module Path: splunkjs/mvc/savedsearchmanager
Default Variable: SavedSearchManager
JavaScript Object instantiation
      Var mySavedSearchManager = new SavedSearchManager({
          id: "savedsearch1",
      searchname: "Saved Report 1"
          "dispatch.earliest_time": "-24h@h",
          "dispatch.latest_time": "now",
          preview: true,
          cache: true
      });
```

The only two required properties are `id` and `searchname`. Both of those must be present in order for this manager to run correctly. The other options are very similar to the SearchManager, except for the dispatch options. The SearchManager has the option `earliest_time`, whereas the SavedSearchManager uses the option `dispatch.earliest_time`. They both have the same restriction but are named differently. The additional options are listed in the main documentation page available at `http://docs.splunk.com/DocumentationStatic/WebFramework/1.1/compref_savedsearchmanager.html`.

PostProcessManager

The **PostProcessManager** does just that, post processes the results of a main search. This works in the same way as the post processing done in SimpleXML; a main search to load the event set, and a secondary search to perform an additional analysis and transformation. Using this manager has its own performance considerations as well. By loading a single job first, and then performing additional commands on those results, you avoid having concurrent searches for the same information. Your usage of CPU and RAM will be less, as you only store one copy of the results, instead of multiple:

```
Module Path: splunkjs/mvc/postprocessmanager
Default Variable: PostProcessManager
JavaScript Object instantiation
    Var mysecondarySearch = new PostProcessManager({
        id: "after_search1",
      search: "stats count by sourcetype",
   managerid: "search1"
        });
```

The `id` property is the only required property. The module won't do anything when instantiated with only an `id` property, but you can set it up to populate later. The other options are similar to the SearchManager, the major difference being that the `search` property in this case is appended to the `search` property of the manager listed in the `managerid` property. For example, if the manager search is `search index=_internal source=*splunkd.log`, and the PostProcessManager search is `stats count by host`, then the entire search for the PostProcessManager is `search index=_internal source=*splunkd.log | stats count by host`. The additional options are listed at the main documentation page at `http://docs.splunk.com/DocumentationStatic/WebFramework/1.1/compref_postprocessmanager.html`.

View-related modules

These modules are related to the views and data visualizations that are native to Splunk. They range in use from charts that display data, to control groups, such as radio groups or dropdowns. These are also included with Splunk and are included by default in the RequireJS declaration.

ChartView

The ChartView displays a series of data in the formats in the list as follows. The following code snippet shows an example of how each different chart is described and presented. Each ChartView is instantiated in the same way, the only difference is in what searches are used with which chart:

```
Module Path:  splunkjs/mvc/chartview
Default Variable: ChartView
JavaScript Object instantiation
        Var myBarChart = new ChartView({
            id: "myBarChart",
            managerid: "searchManagerId",
            type: "bar",
            el: $("#mybarchart")
        });
```

The only required property is the `id` property. This assigns the object an ID that can be later referenced as needed. The `el` option refers to the HTML element in the page that this view will be assigned and created within. The `managerid` relates to an existing search, saved search, or PostProcessManager object. The results are passed from the manager into the chart view and displayed as indicated. Each chart view can be customized extensively using the `charting.*` properties. For example, `charting.chart.overlayFields`, when set to a comma-separated list of field names, will overlay those fields over the chart of other data, making it possible to display SLA times over the top of customer service metrics. The full list of configurable options can be found at `http://docs.splunk.com/Documentation/Splunk/latest/Viz/ChartConfigurationReference`.

The different types of ChartView

Now that we've introduced the ChartView module, let's look at the different types of charts that are built-in. This section has been presented in the following format:

- Name of the chart
- Short description of the chart type
- Type property for use in the JavaScript configuration

- Example chart command that can be displayed with this chart type
- Example image of the chart

The different ChartView types we will cover in this section include the following.

Area

The area chart is similar to the line chart, and compares quantitative data. The graph is filled with color to show volume. This is commonly used to show statistics of data over time.

An example of an area chart is as follows:

```
timechart span=1h max(results.collection1{}.meh_clicks) as
MehClicks max(results.collection1{}.visitors) as Visits
```

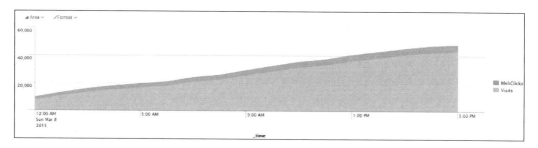

Bar

The bar chart is similar to the column chart except that the x and y axes have been switched, and the bars run horizontally and not vertically. The bar chart is used to compare different categories.

An example of a bar chart is as follows:

```
stats max(results.collection1{}.visitors) as Visits
max(results.collection1{}.meh_clicks) as MehClicks by
results.collection1{}.title.text
```

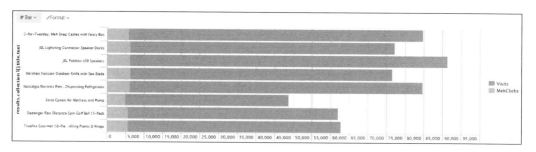

Column

The column chart is similar to the bar chart, but the bars are displayed vertically.

An example of a column chart is as follows:

```
timechart span=1h avg(DPS) as "Difference in Products Sold"
```

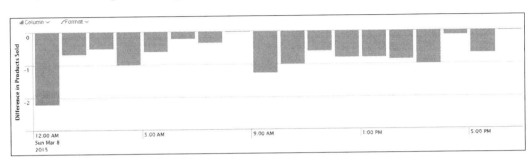

Filler gauge

The filler gauge is a Splunk-provided visualization. It is intended for single values, normally as a percentage, but can be adjusted to use discrete values as well. The gauge uses different colors for different ranges of values, by default using green, yellow, and red, in that order. These colors can also be changed using the charting.* properties. One of the differences between this gauge and the other single value gauges is that it shows both the color and value close together, whereas the others do not.

An example of a filler gauge chart is as follows:

```
eval diff = results.collection1{}.meh_clicks /
results.collection1{}.visitors * 100 | stats latest(diff)
as D
```

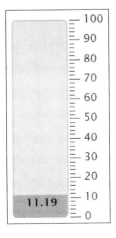

Line

The line chart is similar to the area chart but does not fill the area under the line. This chart can be used to display discrete measurements over time.

An example of a line chart is as follows:

```
timechart span=1h max(results.collection1{}.meh_clicks) as
MehClicks max(results.collection1{}.visitors) as Visits
```

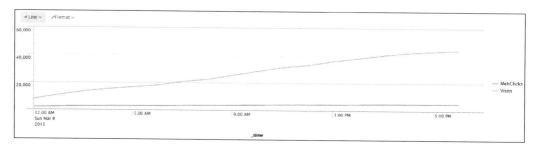

Marker gauge

The marker gauge is a Splunk native visualization intended for use with a single value. Normally, this will be a percentage of a value, but can be adjusted as needed. The gauge uses different colors for different ranges of values, by default using green, yellow, and red, in that order. These colors can also be changed using the charting.* properties.

An example of a marker gauge chart is as follows:

```
eval diff = results.collection1{}.meh_clicks /
results.collection1{}.visitors * 100 | stats latest(diff) as D
```

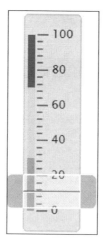

Pie chart

A pie chart is useful for displaying percentages. It gives you the ability to quickly see which part of the *pie* is disproportionate to the others. Actual measurements may not be relevant.

An example of a pie chart is as follows:

```
top op_action
```

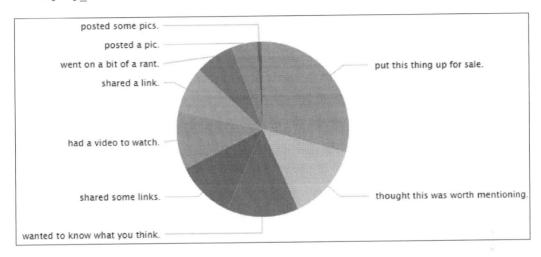

Radial gauge

The radial gauge is another single value chart provided by Splunk. It is normally used to show percentages, but can be adjusted to show discrete values. The gauge uses different colors for different ranges of values, by default using green, yellow, and red, in that order. These colors can also be changed using the charting.* properties.

An example of a radial gauge is as follows:

```
eval diff = MC / V * 100 | stats latest(diff) as D
```

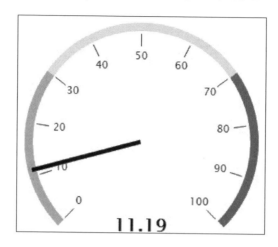

Scatter

The scatter plot can plot two sets of data on an *x* and *y* axis chart (Cartesian coordinates). This chart is primarily time independent and is useful for finding correlations (but not necessarily causation) in data.

An example of a scatter plot is as follows:

```
table MehClicks Visitors
```

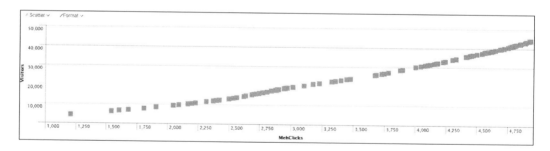

Display-related modules

The following are some display-related modules at our disposal.

CheckboxView

The CheckboxView displays an HTML checkbox, and its value can be retrieved as a Boolean value to indicate whether or not it is checked (true/false). Using tokenization (we will discuss this later in this chapter), you can have the check/ uncheck action trigger a refresh of panels and other views within the dashboard.

The only required options are the `id` and `el` properties, as you have to define where the checkbox will be displayed:

```
Module Path:  splunkjs/mvc/checkboxview
Default Variable: CheckboxView
JavaScript Object instantiation
        new CheckboxView({
              id: "myCheckbox",
              el: "#checkboxview"
        }, {tokens: true, tokenNamespace: "submitted"}).render();
```

CheckboxGroupView

The CheckboxGroupView displays a group of HTML checkboxes, and each item's value can be retrieved as a Boolean value to indicate whether or not it is checked (true/false). Using tokenization, you can have the check/uncheck action trigger a refresh of panels and other views within the dashboard.

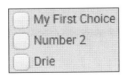

The only required options are the `id` and `el` properties, as you have to define where the checkbox will be displayed. This group of checkboxes can be generated from a search result by defining the `managerid` property. When defining `managerid`, make sure to specify the `labelField` and `valueField` properties, as those will map the search results into your checkbox group:

```
Module Path:  splunkjs/mvc/checkboxgroupview
Default Variable: CheckboxGroupView
JavaScript Object instantiation
        new CheckboxGroupView({
              id: "myCheckboxGroup",
              choices: [
```

```
        {label: "My First Choice", value: "1"},
        {label:" Number 2", value: "2"},
        {label:" Drie", value: "3"}],
        el: $("#checkboxgroupview")
    }, {tokens: true, tokenNamespace: "submitted"}).render();
```

DropdownView

The DropdownView probably does what you think; it displays an HTML drop-down menu with a list of choices. The choices can be static or generated from a SearchManager. When defining `managerid`, make sure to specify the `labelField` and `valueField` properties, as those will map the search results into your drop-down view.

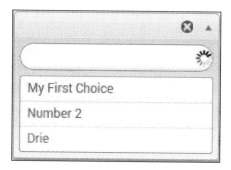

The only required options are the `id` and `el` properties, as you have to define where the drop-down will be displayed:

```
Module Path:    splunkjs/mvc/dropdownview
Default Variable: DropdownView
JavaScript Object instantiation
        new DropdownView({
    id: "dropdownview",
    choices: [
            {label: "My First Choice", value: "1"},
            {label:" Number 2", value: "2"},
            {label:" Drie", value: "3"}],
            el: $("#dropdownview")
        }, {tokens: true, tokenNamespace: "submitted"}).render();
```

EventsViewerView

The EventsViewerView displays the raw events of a SearchManager and includes pagination and formatting. The only required options are the `id` and `el` properties, as you have to define where the events will be displayed. Using the `click` event handlers, you can even trigger the framework to do other actions when an event is clicked. This view has a `type` value that defines how the events are displayed, with the default being `list`:

```
Module Path:  splunkjs/mvc/eventviewview
Default Variable: EventsViewer
JavaScript Object instantiation
        new EventsViewer({
            id: "eventviewer",
            managerid: "mySearchManager",
            type: "table",
            el: "#eventviewer"
        }).render();
```

Once the view has been instantiated, the events will display much like in the following screenshot:

i		Time	Event

>	1	3/9/15 8:29:41.000 AM	`{ [-]`
			`    deal: { [+]`
			`    }`
			`    poll: { [+]`
			`    }`
			`    timestamp: Mon, 09 Mar 2015 08:29:41 EDT`
			`    video: { [+]`
			`    }`
			`}`
			Show as raw text
			host = **splunkerific** source = **meh** sourcetype = **meh**

FooterView

The FooterView displays the Splunk page footer. The only required options are the id and el properties:

```
Module Path:    splunkjs/mvc/footerview
Default Variable: FooterView
JavaScript Object instantiation
        new FooterView({
            id: "myfooter",
            el: "#splunkfooter"
        }).render();
```

Once the view has been instantiated, the events will display much like in the following screenshot:

HeaderView

The HeaderView displays the Splunk page header. The header includes the App selection drop-down, the user menus to navigate to **Settings** and other Splunk items, and the navigation bar for the App. The only required options are the id and el properties:

```
Module Path:    splunkjs/mvc/headerview
Default Variable: HeaderView
JavaScript Object instantiation
        new HeaderView({
            id: "myheader",
            el: "#splunkheader"
        }).render();
```

Once the view has been instantiated, the events will display much like in the following screenshot:

MultiDropdownView

The MultiDropdownView displays an HTML multi-select form item. This allows you to select multiple options and use those values in other functions. The only required options are the `id` and `el` properties, as you have to define where the drop-down will be displayed. The choices can be static or generated from a SearchManager. When defining `managerid`, make sure to specify the `labelField` and `valueField` properties, as those will map the search results into your MultiDropdownView:

```
Module Path:   splunkjs/mvc/multidropdownview
Default Variable: MultiDropdownView
JavaScript Object instantiation
        new MultiDropdownView({
    id: "multidropdownview",
    choices: [
            {label: "My First Choice", value: "1"},
            {label:" Number 2", value: "2"},
            {label:" Drie", value: "3"}],
            el: $("#multidropdownview")
    },   {tokens: true, tokenNamespace: "submitted"}).render();
```

Once the view has been instantiated, the events will display much like in the following screenshot:

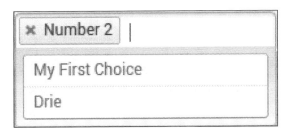

RadioGroupView

The RadioGroupView displays an HTML radio group form item. This allows you to select a single value and use that value in other functions. The only required options are the `id` and `el` properties, as you have to define where the radio group will be displayed. The choices can be static, or generated from a SearchManager. When defining `managerid`, make sure to specify the `labelField` and `valueField` properties, as those will map the search results into your RadioGroupView:

```
Module Path:   splunkjs/mvc/radiogroupview
Default Variable: RadioGroupView
JavaScript Object instantiation
        new RadioGroupView({
```

```
        id: "radiogroupview",
        choices: [
                {label: "My First Choice", value: "1"},
                {label:" Number 2", value: "2"},
                {label:" Drie", value: "3"}],
                el: $("#radiogroupview")
        },  {tokens: true, tokenNamespace: "submitted"}).render();
```

Once the view has been instantiated, the events will display much like in the following screenshot:

SearchBarView

The SearchBarView places the default search bar and time range picker in the element specified. The only required options are the id and el properties, as you have to define where the search bar will be displayed. When instantiated as follows, the search bar won't actually make changes to its SearchManager. You have to use tokenization and change listeners to trigger the automatic reload of other Splunk views:

```
Module Path:    splunkjs/mvc/searchbarview
Default Variable: SearchBarView
JavaScript Object instantiation
        new SearchBarView({
            id: "searchbarview",
            el: $("#searchbarview")
        }).render();
```

Once the view has been instantiated, the events will display much like in the following screenshot:

```
index=splunk_developers_guide sourcetype=meh    All time ∨    🔍
earliest=@d
  ∨
```

SearchControlsView

The SearchControlsView displays the default search controls for a query. This view includes the **Job** drop-down for job-related activities, the **Smart Mode** drop-down (for verbose, smart, or fast search modes), and controls to pause and stop the bound search. The only required options are the id and el properties, as you have to define where the controls will be displayed:

```
Module Path:  splunkjs/mvc/searchcontrolsview
Default Variable: SearchControlsView
JavaScript Object instantiation
      new SearchControlsView({
          id: "searchcontrolsview",
          el: $("#searchcontrolsview")
      }).render();
```

Once the view has been instantiated, the events will display much like in the following screenshot:

SimpleSplunkView

The SimpleSplunkView is special. This is not a directly instantiable view. This is a base class that must be extended (for example, with a custom D3 visualization) for the view to work. We will cover more on extending the SimpleSplunkView in later chapters.

SingleView

The SingleView generates an HTML object with a single value formatted in it. The only required options are the id and el properties, as you have to define where the single value will be displayed. In order to use this effectively, I recommend using a PostProcessManager to narrow down the results to a single value. This helps keep the value at exactly what you need it to be. You can also add a before label and an after label—this displays the text you specify either before or … wait for it … after the value:

```
Module Path:  splunkjs/mvc/singleview
Default Variable: SingleView
JavaScript Object instantiation
      new SingleView({
          id: "singleview",
          field: "count",
```

```
        afterLabel: "count",
        el: "#singleview"
    }).render();
```

Once the view has been instantiated, the events will display much like in the following screenshot:

120   count

MapElement

The MapElement displays a full geographical map of the world, displaying the field values you choose using the `geostats` command. It is recommended that you use the `geostats` command to generate the appropriate dataset for the map. The only required options are the `id` and `el` properties, as you have to define where the map will be displayed:

```
Module Path:   splunkjs/mvc/simplexml/element/map
Default Variable: MapElement
JavaScript Object instantiation
        new MapElement({
            id: "mapElement",
            managerid: "smvppm",
            mapping.type: "marker",
            el: $("#mapelement")
        }).render();
```

Once the view has been instantiated, the events will display much like in the following screenshot:

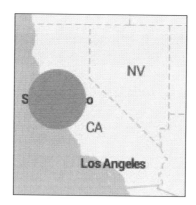

New in Splunk 6.3, you now have the ability to create choropleth maps. These are maps in which you define geometric regions and then map your data to these regions. The instantiation is similar to the marker map, but with a different map type:

```
JavaScript Object instantiation
        new MapElement({
            "id": "mapelement",
            "managerid": "smvppm",
            "mapping.type" : "choropleth",
            "el": $("#mapelement")
        }).render();
```

The data should arrive in the same way using the geostats command, and you will need to use a geo_lookup file to generate and display the data.

TableView

The TableView displays a formatted table of search results. The only required options are the id and el properties, as you have to define where the table will be displayed:

```
Module Path:  splunkjs/mvc/tableview
Default Variable: TableView
JavaScript Object instantiation
        new TableView({
            id: "tableview",
            managerid: "smvppm",
            el: $("#tableview")
        }).render();
```

Once the view has been instantiated, the events will display much like in the following screenshot:

geobin ↕	latitude ↕	longitude ↕
bin_id_zl_0_y_5_x_1	37.78305	-122.39107
bin_id_zl_1_y_11_x_2	37.78305	-122.39107
bin_id_zl_2_y_22_x_5	37.78305	-122.39107
bin_id_zl_3_y_45_x_10	37.78305	-122.39107
bin_id_zl_4_y_90_x_20	37.78305	-122.39107
bin_id_zl_5_y_181_x_40	37.78305	-122.39107

TextInputView

The TextInputView displays an HTML text input box that is commonly used in the forms of dashboards. This form input takes advantage of tokenization and can be used to direct the SearchManagers that are configured. The only required options are the id and el properties, as you have to define where the text box will be displayed:

```
Module Path:   splunkjs/mvc/textinputview
Default Variable: TextInputView
JavaScript Object instantiation
      new TextInputView({
      id: "textinputview",
      el: $("#textinputview")
    }).render();
```

Once the view has been instantiated, the events will display much like in the following screenshot:

TimeRangeView

The TimeRangeView displays a native Splunk view that has the preset values for time ranges. The only required options are the id and el properties, as you have to define where the time range view will be displayed:

```
Module Path:   splunkjs/mvc/timerangeview
Default Variable: TimeRangeView
JavaScript Object instantiation
      new TimeRangeView({
          id: "timerangeview",
          el: $("#timerangeview")
      }).render();
```

Once the view has been instantiated, the events will display much like in the following screenshot:

TimelineView

The TimelineView displays a standard Splunk timeline, with bars representing the number of events within a specified time range. The only required options are the `id` and `el` properties, as you have to define where the timeline view will be displayed:

```
Module Path:  splunkjs/mvc/timelineview
Default Variable: TimelineView
JavaScript Object instantiation
        new TimelineView({
                id: "timelineview",
                managerid: "pollraw",
                el: $("#timelineview")
        }).render();
```

Once the view has been instantiated, the events will display much like in the following screenshot:

Tokenization

Tokenization refers to the use of tokens within a dashboard. A token is a placeholder for a value within a dashboard. These placeholders can be dynamically updated within the dashboard. Searches and other objects can access these values using a special syntax. The basic syntax is to surround the token variable name with $. So, for example, if you defined a TextInputView earlier, and assigned it the token name `myText`, then you would reference the value as `$myText$`.

There are a few different ways to generate token values within a dashboard. These generally include ways to do the following:

- Define tokens to capture input values for forms.
- Define tokens to specify conditional actions based on the value of the token.
- Define tokens within a search string that use values based on previously defined tokens.
- Splunk Enterprise defines token values that you can access. Defined tokens include tokens for visualizations, time inputs, and labels and values of form inputs.

Okay, so now what? Once you have defined a token for use, you need to consume it. You can use these tokens anywhere you would like to, which helps display your data as you see fit. In order to use a token in JavaScript, you must define it in a particular syntax. For example, if you have a `.json` object with the key called `foo`, and you want to dynamically define that term from other parts of the page, you will need to set the value of that key to be token safe, such as `myJson{ "foo": mvc.tokenSafe("$myText$")`. This will bind the value of `myText` to that location, and any time the page uses that token, the value will either be set or retrieved depending on the circumstance.

So, based on our previous discussions on JavaScript views, let's apply a token to the TextInputView, as shown in the following code:

```
new TextInputView({
    id: "myNextText",
    value: mvc.tokenSafe("$goandgetthem$"),
    el: $("#myNext")
}).render();

new SearchManager({
    id: "vpnConn",
    search: mvc.tokenSafe("index=<your vpn index> $goandgetthem$ ")
});
```

As you can see, the value of the drop-down is now bound to the `$goandgetthem$` token, such that any time the token is updated, so is the search, and it will reexecute the search with the new value plugged into it.

Customizing Splunk dashboards using CSS

Now that we have covered the different types of JavaScript modules, let's start customizing our Overview dashboard. We already converted a SimpleXML dashboard to an HTML dashboard, but now we want to add some specific styling. We start by creating a dashboard CSS file in the `appserver/static` folder of our app. In this file, we will override specific Splunk CSS styles, as well as add a few of our own later on, specifically for a D3 visualization. Inside the `dashboard.css` file, add this CSS code:

```
.dashboard-row .dashboard-panel   {
  border: 1px dashed black;
}
```

This CSS will add a dashed border, 1 pixel in width, to each panel in the dashboard, overriding the native Splunk style. Now that we have a CSS file, we need to include it on the page. In order to override the Splunk CSS, you have to place the CSS include after the Bootstrap CSS included with Splunk. This is as simple as placing the code line following this paragraph before the closing head tag `</head>` of the HTML dashboard. There are two ways to edit the HTML dashboard. The first is by using the built-in editor. Located at the top-right of the dashboard, there is a drop-down with the **Edit Source** item. Clicking on that brings you to a web-based interface that allows you to edit the source of the dashboard. There are advantages to using the built-in editor. Primarily, the easiest advantage is not having to refresh the debug endpoint.

 If you edit any of the files under the `appserver/static` page without the built-in editor, then you will have to trigger the debug/refresh endpoint to load the changes.

Let's take a look at the HTML:

```
<link rel="stylesheet" type="text/css"
href="{{SPLUNKWEB_URL_PREFIX}}/static/app/SDG/dashboard.css" />
```

Let's look at the `href` and decode it a little. We have already discussed the `{{SPLUNKWEB_URL_PREFIX}}` variable, which leaves us with the static folder /`static/app/SDG`. This static folder maps to the `appserver/static` folder located within the directory structure of the app. If needed, you can also define a custom directory structure and place the JavaScript and CSS custom files in separate folders. This may help with keeping a multitude of CSS files and JavaScript separate and organized. Once the page is refreshed, your dashboard cells will look like the following. Notice the now dashed borders:

Total Revenue	12m ago	Total Products Sold	12m ago	Average Product Price	12m ago	Average Product Sold per Item	12m ago	Average Revenue per Item	12m ago
s 1362912		≠ 71659		s 45.51		≠ 1378		s 25715.32	

This is a different look, so let's continue to change the entire section to be a single dashboard cell. This will eliminate the space between the cells, giving the dashboard a more cohesive look. Drop down the **Edit** button and hit **Edit Source**. The first part of each panel is coded as follows. We need to change this to make each panel consolidated into the main (or first) panel:

```
<div id="panel1" class="dashboard-cell" style="width: 20%;">
        <div class="dashboard-panel clearfix">
            <div class="panel-element-row">
```

By default, Bootstrap is included with each HTML dashboard. It is very simple to leverage the grid system as you wish. See more about Bootstrap at `http://getbootstrap.com/examples/grid`.

To place each panel in a single panel, remove each of the `div` tags that have the `dashboard-panel clearfix` class. The final result will have a single `div` tag, in this case with the ID `panel1`, and five `div` tags within it that have the `panel-element-row` class. We can't just stop there, as this will put the panels in a vertical orientation. Each panel you transferred will be stacked on top of each other using the default CSS. To change this into a horizontal layout, we created the new `inline-panel` CSS class and added it to `dashboard.css` that we changed earlier:

```
.dashboard-row .dashboard-panel .inline-panel {
        display: inline-block;
        width: 19%;
        vertical-align: bottom;
        text-align: center;
}
```

Note how we included both `dashboard-row` and `dashboard-panel`. This helps to target the CSS, limiting it to only dashboard panels. Now that we added this CSS to the `dashboard.css` file, we need to hit the debug/refresh endpoint. Once that finishes loading, you can reload the Overview dashboard and see how the changes are rendered:

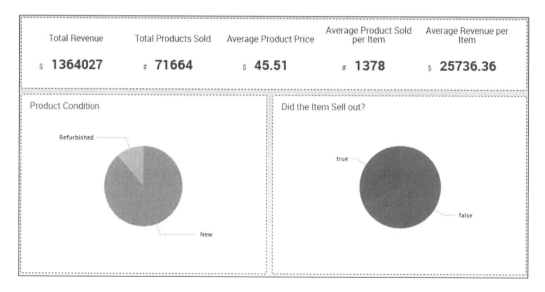

See how that changes the dashboard? Instead of five distinct values displayed, we now have five related values displayed. It helps to focus the end user's eye and eliminates the gray space between values. The charts are still separated with a gray space but since the two charts are not directly related, we don't need to put them in the same panel. This is a very simple example, but it shows you how easy it is to modify the existing classes and add your own to create new and visually explosive dashboards. The full power of CSS can be unleashed into your app.

Customizing Splunk dashboards using JavaScript

Before we start using custom JavaScript, let's work with the already included JavaScript to make our dashboard include animation. In this example, we will add additional controls to each chart to allow them to slide. This is advantageous in that you can give the user control to hide charts they are not interested in, or that take up too much space to see the charts they want to examine.

Firstly, let's add the slide controls. Right after the `panel-element-row` div tag for the two charts, you will see a `panel-head` div tag. After the `panel-head` div tag, you will see a `dashboard-element` div tag. The concept here is to use the header as the slide control, thereby leaving the header visible and allowing the end user to notice that there might be more information. In order to achieve this, you must move the header before the element. The default code shows the header contained within the `div` element:

```
<div id="element6" class="dashboard-element chart"
style="width: 100%">
  <div class="panel-head">
        <h3>Product Condition</h3>
      </div>
      <div class="panel-body"></div>
</div>
```

The following modified code shows how we need to set up the `div` tags in order to achieve the slide control:

```
<div class="panel-head" id="element6slideControl">
  <h3>Product Condition</h3>
</div>
<div id="element6" class="dashboard-element chart"
style="width: 100%">
  <div class="panel-body"></div>
</div>
```

The header is now located before the element chart. The only other modification needed to the header `div` is to add an `id` attribute. This will give the JavaScript an element to bind to. Since our `slideToggle` function is native within jQuery (which is already included by default), we don't need to include a custom JavaScript file. To add the slide functionality, navigate within the HTML source code of the dashboard until you find the `Dashboard Ready` section. This section is labeled with a comment (if you converted from SimpleXML to HTML using the built-in conversion process). Right before that section, add this JavaScript code:

```
$("#element6slideControl").click(function(){
        $("#element6").slideToggle("slow");
        $("#panel6").resize();
        element6.render();
    });


$("#element7slideControl").click(function(){
        $("#element7").slideToggle("slow");
        $("#panel7").resize();
        element7.render();
    });
```

Save your dashboard. Once the dashboard completes loading, it looks like nothing has changed. However, in fact, you can now click on the header for the chart, and voila! It disappears. Now your dashboard can look like the following one, allowing more data to be placed into a smaller place.

Total Revenue <1m ago	Total Products Sold <1m ago	Average Product Price <1m ago	Average Product Sold per Item <1m ago	Average Revenue per Item <1m ago
$ 1365142	# 71669	$ 45.51	# 1378	$ 25757.40

Product Condition	Did the Item Sell out?

This method can be applied for any of the built-in jQuery functions, since, by default, jQuery is included on the page.

Now let's add some custom JavaScript! Custom JavaScript is included in much the same way as CSS, but the placement within the page will depend on how the JavaScript will be used. RequireJS modules as well as generic functions can be included. The standard format on how to use a `<script>` tag is available to add custom JavaScript. The most likely place for the inclusion statement would be directly before the JavaScript that includes the SplunkJS library.

For this example, we will add a simple function to the dashboard. This function (shown as follows) will take a string and return it formatted with a comma to separate the thousands place:

```
function numberWithCommas(x) {
    return x.toString().replace(/\B(?=(\d{3})+(?!\d))/g, ",");
}
```

This function is contained within the `dashboard.js` file in `appserver/static`. Once the file is created, it must be included. Locate the line in your dashboard that includes `simplexml.min/config.js` into the dashboard. After this line, you will add the additional JavaScript files that are needed. Let's add ours:

```
<script src="{{SPLUNKWEB_URL_PREFIX}}/static/app/SDG/dashboard.js" />
```

Simple enough, right? Now we have to use it, which is simple as well. Once it is included on the page, you can use it anywhere after the inclusion. We won't spend time trying this out; there is a much better way to include libraries into the dashboard. jQuery is by default included in the dashboard; it is a founding framework for the Splunk Web Framework.

However, let's say you want to include a jQuery plugin. How would you do that? Since Splunk uses RequireJS, the answer is simple: use RequireJS. Let's add a plugin called **sidr**. This is a side or top slide-in/out plugin. You can find it online at `https://github.com/artberri/sidr`. Download the library and unzip it in the `appserver/static` folder. Notice how we are starting to collect quite a few CSS and JavaScript files? Let's make two new folders: `css` and `js`. Move the CSS file for sidr into the `css` folder and the JS file for sidr into the `js` folder. Once they are in place, edit the dashboard and include the CSS file:

```
<link rel="stylesheet" type="text/css"
href="{{SPLUNKWEB_URL_PREFIX}}/static/app/SDG/css/jquery.sidr.dark.
css" />
```

Now we need an element to place the slide into. Add it underneath the dashboard header:

```
<a id="simple-menu" href="#sidr">Toggle menu</a>
<div id="sidr"><div id="sidr_content">
</div>
```

Next, we include the jQuery plugin JavaScript file using RequireJS. Find the section that has the `require.config` section. Replace the default section with this code:

```
var AppBase = "{{SPLUNKWEB_URL_PREFIX}}/static/app/SDG/js";
require.config({
        baseUrl: "{{SPLUNKWEB_URL_PREFIX}}/static/js",
        paths : {
                "sidr": AppBase + "/jquery.sidr.min"
            },
        shim : { "sidr" : { deps: ["jquery"] }},
    waitSeconds: 0 // Disable require.js load timeout
});
```

Let's review the changes. The `AppBase` variable points to the base JavaScript folder within the app. Although not required, the `AppBase` variable is nonetheless helpful, especially when you have multiple plugins that are required. In the `paths` object, you can see where we specify the path to the JavaScript file that we downloaded earlier. The object field name `sidr` is used as a reference to the path in later configurations. Next up is the `shim` object. A `shim` allows you to define dependencies between libraries. The general configuration syntax is `"PATH_NAME" : { deps: [ ARRAY OF PATH_NAMES ] }`, with one object per dependency requirement. sidr requires jQuery, and since jQuery is included with Splunk, we can reference the native name.

Next, find the `require` function (typically right after the config) and find the array of libraries and modules. Add `sidr` at the end; it should look something like this:

```
"splunkjs/mvc/simplexml/urltokenmodel",
"sidr"
```

This will load the sidr library, only after its dependencies are loaded. The other item required is the variable to assign the library to. In the next section, find the end of the variable list and add a variable name that is descriptive:

```
UrlTokenModel,
Sidr
```

We named it `Sidr`. This is now a JavaScript variable that contains the library. Since this is a jQuery plugin, we will be able to use it like a jQuery plugin. Instantiation is easy now. Find the location in the JavaScript under `pageLoading = true`. Add this code: `$("#simple-menu").sidr();`. Then, save the dashboard; but wait, where did it go? Well, it's hidden. Find the **Toggle menu** link at the top of the dashboard and click on it. The panel is displayed! Awesome! Just that simply, we can add additional jQuery plugins and other JavaScript. Here is our end product; we added a table with the latest sales stats as a quick reference.

See the download link for the code that was used to create this content. Make sure you use visually appealing configurations, such as an icon, for slide outs! People can quickly recognize them and don't have to search for text:

Product	Ooma Telo Air Classic with Wireless Adapter (Refurbished)
Meh Clicks	5319
Visitors	50454
% Didn't Fall for It	99.53
Items Sold	268
Total Revenue	18313

Custom D3 visualization

Now that we have a slide-out, let's move on to visualizations. We now want to add an information graphic that displays some statistics about the prices of the products. So, let's use a box plot! D3 offers a nice example at `http://bl.ocks.org/mbostock/4061502`. We will take this code and adapt it for use with this dashboard. Let's start with the CSS for the box plots. This is located in the `index.html` section of the tutorial. Copy all the CSS except for the `body` class to the `dashboard.css` file in the App. In that same section, find the `irq` function, and copy that into the `dashboard.js` file. Now, find the `box.js` section. Copy the entire function to a file under `appserver/static/js`. Download and place a copy of `d3.min.js` in `appserver/static/js`. Once these files are in place, add them to the RequireJS stack using the methods described in the last section. D3 won't have a dependency but the box plot requires D3. This completes the initial dependency setup for the visualization. Now we can move onto the meat of the visualization.

Firstly, we need a new dashboard panel:

```
<div id="row3" class="dashboard-row dashboard-row3">
    <div id="panel8" class="dashboard-cell" style="width: 100%;">
        <div class="dashboard-panel clearfix">
            <div class="panel-element-row">
                <div class="panel-head">
```

```
                              <h3>Product Metric Comparisons</h3>
                         </div>
                    <div class="dashboard-element chart" style="width:
     100%">
                         <div id="boxPlotElement" style="display:inline-
     block"></div>
                         <div style="display:inline-block;vertical-
     align:top;"><h4>From left to right, the box plots are:</h4><ul>
                              <li>product_price</li>
                                <li>product_sold</li>
                                  <li>product_meh_clicks</li>
                                    <li>product_visitors</li>
                                      <li>product_total_revenue</li>
                              </ul></div>
                         </div>
                    </div>
               </div>
          </div>
     </div>
```

Here, we added a dashboard panel after the two pie charts.

When copying and pasting code, always remember to change the element IDs—or things will break!

Using what we discussed about SearchManagers, let's set one up for the box plot data. Note that the search string isn't shown—it's actually a macro! So, when we want to modify the data, we don't have to change the dashboard—only the macro:

```
     var salesBoxPlotSearch = new SearchManager({
          "id": "salesBoxPlotSearch",
          "search": "|'productBoxPlots'"
     }, {tokens: true, tokenNamespace: "submitted"});
```

Okay, so we have a SearchManager. How the heck do we get the data out of it? Thankfully, Splunk has decided that might be a useful feature, so there is a method to extract the data. We will start with providing the code and then review each part:

```
     var salesBoxPlotResults = salesBoxPlotSearch.data("results");
       salesBoxPlotResults.on("data", function() {
       var d3_data = [];
         var index = 0;
```

```
    _.each(salesBoxPlotResults.data().rows, function(Rcolumn,
RrowCount) {
        Rcolumn.shift();
        _.each(Rcolumn, function(DColumn, DrowCount) {
            d3_data.push( [index, DColumn ]);
        });
        index++;
        //Transform Data into D3 Array
    });
    //D3 Visualization Code
});
```

The first line of this code block retrieves the data from the SearchManager object. The `results` parameter tells Splunk to return the events found from the search in the `results` format, which would match up with the **Results** tab in a typical search. The second line sets a trigger function to execute when the data results are populated. The `data` parameter simply tells Splunk that when there is data present, start executing the code block. Inside this function, we need to massage the data and draw the chart. Massaging the data is necessary to present the data in a format that the D3 visualization can understand and use. Here, we are translating the data into an array of arrays, since this is the expected format for the box plot visualization. The transformed data is now stored into the `d3_data` variable.

This is what the data looks like:

```
[[0,1],[0,3],[0,4],[1,2],[1,5],[1,6]]
```

The first index is the box plot index and the second is the value index. We got this data by tabling the data from the SearchManager. From here, we simply create the D3 element, assign the data, and output into the element we created earlier. The final plot is shown as follows. As you can see, the box plot automatically calculates the min, max, mean, 25th percentile, 75th percentile, and also shows the outliers.

This gives you a distribution of the different fields we analyze:

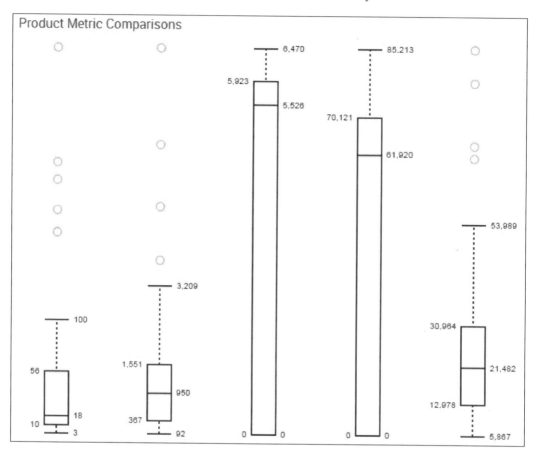

A quick analysis of each field can be done using this chart, for example, looking at the middle chart (which is the number of users who clicked on the **meh** button and is fairly consistent, which can indicate a healthy user community or just a mindless addiction to clicking a button). Either way, these plots can give insight into the behavior of the users. From left to right, the fields are **product price**, **total number of products sold**, **number of Meh button clicks**, **number of visitors to the site**, and **total revenue sold**. The more data you have, the more valuable these graphs become.

External data and content

Very quickly, we will mention ways to pull in additional data from external sources. These can be external data sources, or more likely, internal API calls to internal services.

Data

Say you have an internal monitoring solution that has an API. Since you want to be efficient in both the collection of data and the storage of data, you only want to collect and store the performance data in the internal monitoring solution. However, how can you integrate the API data with the performance data? Simply put, you can build a script input that consumes the API data and stores the resulting performance data in a lookup that you can use to automatically enhance the data. You can also use jQuery to pull that data right into the dashboard and use the D3 visualizations as well as the built-in JavaScript objects to visualize it. This is done quite simply by using the Ajax library of jQuery:

```
$.ajax({
  url: "http://myinternalserver.example.com/getNode/myNode"
})
  .done(function( data ) {
    if ( console && console.log ) {
      console.log( data );
    }
  });
```

Very simply, this performs a GET on the URL provided and returns the data into the done function. From there, you can manipulate it in any way you wish and use it to enhance your dashboard even further.

Content

Including CSS and JS on the page is very simple—although, due to cross-site scripting concerns, it is not recommended. It is very possible to include an iframe on the page, in order to display the latest rendering of the page. You can also include JavaScript libraries and modules from external sources but the browser has to be enabled to allow it since it can be a security risk. There are also performance considerations to consider, so if it is at all possible, download the libraries and modules to the static folder and serve it locally from Splunk.

Summary

In this chapter, we covered some deeper elements of Splunk applications and visualizations. Starting with the basics of HTML dashboards and the Splunk Web Framework, we discussed how to include basic CSS overrides for some of the Splunk CSS. We also covered the static folder location within an app that serves content as needed. We mentioned the use of the bump button to bust open the caches if something isn't rendered properly. After that protip, we reviewed each of the SplunkJS modules, how to instantiate them, and gave an example of each. Moving right along, we reviewed how to set tokens within the dashboard, and how to trigger changes in the display based on updates to the tokens. We customized the dashboard with CSS and started including custom JavaScript and D3 visualizations. The method of placing the D3 visualization in the dashboard was neither smooth nor reusable across other dashboards. We will show that configuration in the next chapter. We will cover how to make a custom D3 visualization modular and reusable in multiple dashboards.

Once we were done customizing our dashboard, we took a quick look at the ability to pull information in from external sources. Using these different concepts and code snippets, you can start creating awesome dashboards!

6
Advanced Integrations and Development

In this chapter, we will be discussing additional methods of integration and development. We will start with building a modular D3 visualization, which is an expansion of the D3 visualization from the last chapter. Using modular visualizations allows you to be more flexible with your dashboards and allows you to tweak a particular visualization for all dashboards in which it has been used. We will discuss modular inputs and how to create and test them. Modular inputs allow you to consume the same type of data in a modular fashion, similar to the native directory or file monitoring inputs found in Splunk. We will also cover the KV Store, how to use it, and why to use it. The KV Store allows you to store information in a key-value manner, which has the potential to speed up lookup tables, as the data is stored in the memory. We will also cover how to use Bower, npm, Gulp, and Git as tools for customizing and tracking our apps.

Modular D3 visualization

In this section, we will convert our previously used D3 box plot graph (we added this in *Chapter 5, The Splunk Web Framework*) into extended SimpleSplunkView. The benefits here are substantial. Primarily, you gain the ability to quickly reuse the view in other dashboards. Simply assign the SearchManager to the view and off you go. Retrieving the events from the SearchManager is also easier, as it is handled natively within the extension. Another great benefit is that when the view is loading, the default loading screens are used, so it's not just a blank panel until it is loaded; it is actually a first-class-citizen view. The first thing to have when creating an extended SimpleSplunkView is the base template.

Let's take a look at the basic structure and then fill in the pieces we are missing:

```
define(function(require, exports, module) {
    var _ = require("underscore");
    var mvc = require("splunkjs/mvc");
    var SimpleSplunkView = require
      ("splunkjs/mvc/simplesplunkview");
    var D3BoxPlot = SimpleSplunkView.extend({
        className: "d3boxplot",
        options: {
            data: "preview"
        },
        createView: function() {
            return vis;
        },
        formatData: function(data) {
            return data;
        },
        updateView: function(vis, data) {
        }
    });
    return D3BoxPlot;
});
```

This is the basic template for SimpleSplunkView. It is written as a RequireJS module (remember RequireJS from *Chapter 5, The Splunk Web Framework*?), and you should notice that it references internal Splunk modules. RequireJS is a framework meant for loading JavaScript files and modules. A RequireJS module is written to be included in different parts of an application, allowing you to extend any RequireJS-compatible installation. You can find the documentation and some really awesome examples on their website at http://requirejs.org. The internal Splunk modules are *underscore* and any modules that start with splunkjs. These are already part of the stack, making it easier to import the modules. Once the additional modules are included, you call on the extend function of SimpleSplunkView. The configuration object you are passing includes some functions that are required for a simple Splunk view. "Where does this JavaScript go?" you might ask. Into appserver/static/js, of course! Let's call this file d3boxplotModule.js. There is another important thing to note here. Since we are using D3 as the visualization library, we have to include that library in the view class. Add the following code directly before the SimpleSplunkView require statement:

```
require('../app
/SDG/js/d3.min');
```

Note that SDG here is actually the name of your App. The path is required in this instance because when the file is included in the dashboard, it will call it relative to the page, not the file.

Now give your view a class name relevant to the visualization being presented. Keep it simple; it doesn't have to be a book! Following that is the options configuration. This doesn't have to contain anything, but if it does, you can use these values as defaults within the view. For example, if you want a base height and width, you can define it here. If a new value is passed via the JavaScript instantiation, then your default will be overwritten. Let's now move to the formatData function. This function will take the results being passed in from the assigned SearchManager, format the data into the structure required by the box plot, and return it. Here is what our formatData function will look like:

```
formatData: function(data) {
        var d3_data = [];
        var index = 0;
        _.each(data, function(Rcolumn, RrowCount) {
            Rcolumn.shift();
            _.each(Rcolumn, function(DColumn,
              DrowCount) {
                d3_data.push( [index, DColumn ]); });
                index++;
            });
        var mydata = [];
        var min = Infinity,
            max = -Infinity;

        d3_data.forEach(function(x) {
          var e = Math.floor(x[0]),
              s = Math.floor(x[1]),
              d = mydata[e];
          if (!d) d = mydata[e] = [s];
          else d.push(s);
          if (s > max) max = s;
          if (s < min) min = s;
        });
      return data;
    }
```

This is essentially the same function we used previously in the configuration of the box plot in *Chapter 5, The Splunk Web Framework*. The only major changes were some naming conventions for the data arrays, just to keep inline with the standard module definitions. This function is what does the heavy lifting for the `boxPlot` chart data. Now that we've had the data formatted properly, let's take a look at the `createView` function:

```
createView: function() {
        var iqr = function(k) {
                return function(d, i) {
                var q1 = d.quartiles[0],
                    q3 = d.quartiles[2],
                    iqr = (q3 - q1) * k,
                    i = -1,
                    j = d.length;
                    while (d[++i] < q1 - iqr);
                    while (d[--j] > q3 + iqr);
                    return [i, j];
        }};
        var margin = {top: 10, right: 50, bottom: 20,
          left: 50},
            width = 130 - margin.left - margin.right,
            height = 500 - margin.top - margin.bottom;
        var chart = d3.box()
            .whiskers(iqr(1.5))
            .width(width)
            .height(height);
      return { "chart": chart, "width":width, "height
        ":height, "margin":margin };
    }
```

Again, this looks pretty similar to the code we had earlier for the box plot in *Chapter 5, The Splunk Web Framework,* but with some slight changes. The `iqr` function is now a variable placed inline so that it can be easily referenced for the whiskers of the box plot. This function can be called globally, but since it is limited in scope for us in this view, we just set it as `local`. The other change from the normal function of this function is the `return` object. The chart is returned as an object within an object, which allows easy expansion to other variables as needed on the fly, as the only objects given to the `updateView` function are those returned from this function (`createView`) and the `formatData` function.

Speaking of the `updateView` function, let's take a peek in there:

```
updateView: function(chartObj, data) {
            var width = chartObj.width,
                height = chartObj.height,
                margin = chartObj.margin,
                chart = chartObj.chart;

            console.log("update view");
            d3.select(this.el).selectAll("svg")
                .data(data)
                .enter().append("svg")
                .attr("class", "box")
                .attr("width", width + margin.left +
                  margin.right)
                .attr("height", height + margin.bottom +
                  margin.top)
                .append("g")
                .attr("transform", "translate(" +
                  margin.left + "," + margin.top + ")")
                .call(chart);
    }
```

Yet again, this is basically the same D3 code as we had previously in *Chapter 5, The Splunk Web Framework*, with minor tweaks for modularity. The biggest change is the `d3.select` call is that it now references `this.el`, which was passed in from the instantiation. This is the element that will contain the chart. So, with that change, we can now instantiate multiple box charts in the same dashboard. How? Here's how:

```
var salesBoxPlotResults = new boxPlot({
            el: $('#boxPlotElement'),
            id: "salesBoxPlotResults",
            managerid: "salesBoxPlotSearch"
        }).render();
```

That's it. Now that we've modularized the box plot, as shown in the following diagram, we simply call it using `new boxPlot` (which is the name of our variable after we include the module in RequireJS). Pass in the parameters required and render the visualization.

So simple! It keeps your dashboards clean and easy to read. How does it look? You tell me.

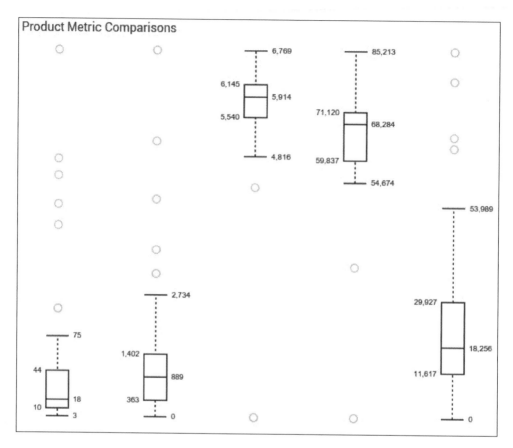

As you can see, it looks identical to what we created in the last chapter, but with the advantage of being *plug and play*. Keep in mind that this is a simple demonstration of how to create a custom view; these can be as simple or as complex as you like. This is far from customizable in terms of coloring, labels, legends, axes, and formatting. Each of these options can be included in the custom view and taken as far as you are able to take them.

However, what about SimpleXML, you ask? It's a very valid question. Including custom visualizations into SimpleXML dashboards can be very easy, depending on how you choose to implement the code. Splunk's approach uses the `autodiscover.js` methodology; you can learn more about their method from `https://dev.splunk.com`. However, what happens if I want to change the App name? Using the `autodiscover.js` approach will break all the defined dashboards. So, let's add a few things to the `dashboard.js` file in `appserver/static`. Let's start with a configuration for RequireJS:

```
var APPNAME = "SDG";
require.config({
  paths: {
    "boxplot": "../app/"+APPNAME+"/js/d3boxPlot",
    "d3": "../app/"+APPNAME+"/js/d3.min"
  },
  shim: {
    "d3":{exports:"d3"},
    "boxplot" : { deps: ["d3"] }
  }
});
```

The preceding code starts up by creating some configurations needed to point to the correct location. With a simple change of the APPNAME variable, all references to the App's name will change, and all the custom visualizations using this method in the dashboards will work again. Simple! Now for some magic!

```
require([    "splunkjs/ready!",    "splunkjs/mvc/simplexml/ready!",
"jquery",    "underscore",    "boxplot"],
function(    mvc,    ignored,    $,    _,    boxPlot) {
    $(".boxPlot").each(function(index){
        el = $(this);
        data = el.data();
        data["el"] = el;
        new boxPlot(data).render();
    });
});
```

This section of code does a very simple thing. It uses jQuery to find each element with the specific class `boxPlot`. For each such element that is found, we will use the `data()` function of each element to pull the required configuration settings. Let's look at an example of the HTML element to use to support this instantiation method. The really important part is the HTML `div`, and it can be used in either the SimpleXML or the HTML dashboard:

```
<panel>
    <html>
        <div class="boxPlot" data-managerid="mySearch"></div>
    </html>
</panel>
```

The `data-managerid` attribute will be parsed to the item of `managerid`. This makes it clean and easy to read. For each *option* that is required for the visualization (and that you'd normally include in a messy JSON option in the `data-require` attribute), you place it into a `data-<option>` format. That's it! Now you can define the visualization once and allow your App developers to use a simple `div` class and some options without having to build a JSON object to build the dashboard.

Modular inputs

Modular inputs are a feature of Splunk that allow you to extend the platform in ways that are specifically geared to consuming data. Modular inputs can promote your scripted inputs to first-class natives of the Splunk platform. This gives you the ability to define how to collect the data and let your users define the settings with which to collect that data. "Why would you want that?" you might ask. Lots of reasons! For example, let's say that you want to gather data about the weather. You could write a scripted input to collect a single city's weather data from the API of wunderground. com. However, what happens when you want more than one city's weather data? You'll have to copy and paste the scripted input, change the API parameters, and update the API key. If there was a change made to the API specification, you will have to update all configured scripted inputs. If you use a modular input, you can give the user an option to specify the API key and the API parameters in the Web interface. Once these are specified, Splunk will automatically collect that data using the set options. If any specification changes, you change the modular input code, and then it is changed for every input defined. Much easier to scale! Here are a few more features of modular inputs that can be found at `http://docs.splunk.com/Documentation/Splunk`:

- Splunk Web automatically provides access to your custom-defined inputs.
- You can provide validation for the inputs.

- You can package platform-specific versions of a script; for example, you can include a Windows version, a Linux version, and an Apple (Darwin) version in your package.

- You can stream data as XML data, which allows you to annotate the script output. This gives you greater control over how Splunk Enterprise processes the data.

- You can use Splunk Enterprise REST endpoints to access your modular input scripts.

- You can set permissions for these endpoints using Splunk Enterprise's capabilities.

- You can define whether to launch a single instance or multiple instances. A single instance mode is useful when running in a single-threaded environment.

As you can see, modular inputs give greater flexibility and robustness to your inputs. Now you might ask, "Well when would I use this (in a generic sense)?" The best time to decide whether you need a modular input is when you find yourself writing and rewriting scripted inputs that are all essentially the same, with only slight modifications for configuration items such as usernames, authentication tokens, and/or REST parameters. So, now you know what, why, and when. Let's see how.

We are going to build a very simple REST modular input. This modular input will consume data from a non-authenticating, public API. These APIs are tied to the meh. com forum and product detail pages. The actual APIs are hosted by kimonolabs.com, which allows you to turn any web page into a REST API. Very cool stuff! You should check it out. The reason we are going to build these APIs is that just now (although you didn't know it), we were using two scripted inputs to consume two different APIs. The only real difference is the API URL. Let's abstract the input so that we can update and add new APIs via the GUI. Modular inputs are written in Python, so all code presented, unless specified otherwise, is of Python.

Modular inputs have two different modes, depending on the way they are run. They are the **single script instance per input stanza mode** and **single script instance mode**. The main difference in these modes is how they are executed. In the single script instance per input stanza mode, a new instance (process) will spawn for each defined input. This allows you to set multiple inputs with different intervals (300 seconds versus 900 seconds). In the other mode, single script instance mode, Splunk reads only the scheme's default interval setting. This interval cannot be overridden. More often than not, you will probably use the single script instance per input stanza mode.

The spec file

Let's define the spec file first. This is a new file, in a new folder. The folder is called README and is placed under the root of the App. The file is called inputs.conf. spec. This defines the modular input as an input, while also defining the different configuration options available. Let's put this text into that file:

```
[sdgAPI://default]
* This is the API Modular Input for the Splunk Developers Guide

api_url = <value>
* This is the non-authenticated API URL to consume
```

The stanza for this configuration has the script name sdgAPI. This is what will be referenced in the local inputs.conf files of the App. This also references the name of the script that will be used for the input, sdgAPI.py, located in the bin folder of the App. The next step, after we have our spec file, is to set up the Python script that will actually consume the API that will be configured.

Let's create the sdgAPI.py file in the bin folder.

 When constructing modular inputs, you have to ensure that the name of the Python file is the same as the stanza configuration in the spec file.

So, in this case, we are using sdgAPI. The full text of this code will be available as a download, but we will display the relevant portions to explain some important sections. Not shown are the import statements required for Python, the logging setup, and some general script variables. The first section we will cover is the scheme, and it might look something like this:

```
SCHEME = """<scheme>
    <title>sdgAPI</title>
    <description>Get data from an un-authenticated REST API</
description>
    <use_external_validation>true</use_external_validation>
    <streaming_mode>xml</streaming_mode>
    <endpoint>
        <args>
            <arg name="api_url">
                <title>API URL</title>
                <description>The URL</description>
            </arg>
        </args>
    </endpoint>
```

```
</scheme>
"""

def do_scheme():
    """ Prints the Scheme """
    doPrint(SCHEME)

def doPrint(s):
    """ A wrapper Function to output data by same method (print vs
        sys.stdout.write) """
    sys.stdout.write(s)
```

The scheme should match the spec file exactly. The spec file contains the definitions for each argument. If you have a parameter as `hostname`, the scheme must also have `hostname`. The scheme must be written in XML and presented to the system when asked (this is shown in code a little further on). For each additional argument required from the `input.spec.config`, you must add an `arg` section to the scheme. The `do_scheme` and `doPrint` functions are very simple. The `doPrint` function is just a wrapper meant for writing to the system, but we use it wherever we want to write to the system, which is exactly what printing the scheme is supposed to do. The next step in the modular input is to read the configuration of the modular input. This data is pulled in from the `inputs.conf` file after the modular input is configured through the GUI:

```
#read XML configuration passed from splunkd
def get_config():
    """ Read XML Configuration data passed from splunkd on stdin """
    config = {}
    try:
        # read everything from stdin
        config_str = sys.stdin.read()
        # parse the config XML
        doc = xml.dom.minidom.parseString(config_str)
        root = doc.documentElement
        conf_node = root.getElementsByTagName("configuration")[0]
        if conf_node:
            logging.debug("XML: found configuration")
            stanza = conf_node.getElementsByTagName("stanza")[0]
            if stanza:
                stanza_name = stanza.getAttribute("name")
                if stanza_name:
                    logging.debug("XML: found stanza " +
                        stanza_name)
                    config["name"] = stanza_name
```

```
                    params = stanza.getElementsByTagName("param")
                    for param in params:
                        param_name = param.getAttribute("name")
                        logging.debug("XML: found param '%s'" %
                          param_name)
                        if param_name and param.firstChild and \
                            param.firstChild.nodeType == param.
                              firstChild.TEXT_NODE:
                            data = param.firstChild.data
                            config[param_name] = data
                            logging.debug("XML: '%s' -> '%s'" %
                              (param_name, data))

            if not config:
                raise Exception, "Invalid configuration received from
                    Splunk."
            # just some validation: make sure these keys are present
                (required)
            validate_conf(config, "api_url")
        except Exception, e:
            raise Exception, "Error getting Splunk configuration via
                STDIN: %s" % str(e)
        return config
```

This section of the code reads in the configuration data from `stdin`, which is passed to the script from the `splunkd` process. The function takes the `stdin` configuration data, parses it (it is passed in XML), and builds a Python `list` object with the configuration data. This section of code is important because it also validates the configuration, in this case, using the `validate_conf` function. This is where you determine and enforce which attributes are required. For each configuration option that will be required, add another `validate_conf` call with the appropriate arguments. The next parts of the code will be a review of some functions that I typically use to keep the code a little simpler and standardized:

```
def do_done_event(sourcetype, source):
    """ Outputs a single done even for an unbroken event to the
      Splunk Processor """
    dostr = "<event><source>%s</source><sourcetype>%s
      </sourcetype><done/></event>" % (escape(source),
      escape(sourcetype))
    doPrint(dostr)


def init_stream():
    """ Sends the XML for starting a Stream """
```

```
        logging.debug("Setting up stream")
        doPrint("<stream>")

    def end_stream():
        """ Sends the XML for ending a Stream """
        logging.debug("Ending Stream")
        doPrint("</stream>")

    def getAPIResults(url):
        """ SENDS THE JSON FROM THE API CALL """
        logging.debug("Getting URL: %s"%url)
        request = urllib2.Request(url)
        response = urllib2.urlopen(request)
        return(response.read())
```

Starting off is the do_done_event function. The purpose of this function is to print a done event. Splunk expects XML on stdout, in order to consume and place data in the indexes. This function tells Splunk that we are done sending data and tells it to close the processing. The next functions are init_stream and end_stream. These are crucial for telling Splunk when a stream of data starts and when it ends. You will see in the next section how they are used. The last function in this list is getAPIResults. It takes a single URL as its argument. This is the meat of the modular input. Using the **urllib2** libraries, it opens a connection to the URL, creates the response, and reads the response. The read response is returned to whence it came, in this case into another function, as seen here:

```
    def run():
        """ The Main function that starts the action. The thread will
            sleep for however many seconds are configured via the Input.
        """
        sys.stdout = Unbuffered(sys.stdout)
        config = get_config()
        stanza = config["name"]
        sourcetype = config["sourcetype"]
        source = get_source(stanza[(stanza.rfind("/")+1):])
        init_stream()
        logging.info("source=%s sourcetype=%s stanza=%s operation
            =running_api"%(source,sourcetype,stanza))
        do_event("%s"%(getAPIResults(config["api_url"])),
            sourcetype,source)
        do_done_event(sourcetype,source)
        end_stream()
```

The `run` section is what actually builds the data stream and gets the data. Inside this function, we start with getting the configuration from `stdin`, using the `get_config` function we saw earlier. We then assign some variables, which will be reused multiple times within the data collection process. After that, we initialize the data stream to Splunk by calling `init_stream`, which basically just prints `<stream>` on the `stdout`, where Splunk picks it up. Following `init_stream`, we call `do_event` with the results of the API call as a string. This is what actually gets consumed and stored in Splunk. Once we are done with getting the data from the API, we finish the event (`do_done_event`) and then close the stream with `end_stream`. The only thing left to do now is to call the `run` function:

```
if __name__ == '__main__':
    if len(sys.argv) > 1:
        if sys.argv[1] == "--scheme":
            do_scheme()
        elif sys.argv[1] == "--validate-arguments":
            validate_arguments()
        elif sys.argv[1] == "--test":
            doPrint('No tests for the scheme present')
        else:
            doPrint('You giveth weird arguments')
    else:
        run()

    sys.exit(_SYS_EXIT_OK)
```

This is a standard Python statement. It is the first thing that is executed within the script. We need it to support introspection and argument validation. If Splunk passes `--scheme`, the scheme is printed using `do_scheme`. Arguments are validated by passing `--validate-arguments`. If there are no system arguments, then the `run` function is called and off we go! These are some basic building blocks for a modular input. Full code examples are available online in the Splunk documentation. Once you are done with writing your code, you can move on to testing and integration.

Testing modular inputs

Testing is very important, since without testing, how do you know it will work? Testing modular inputs is pretty simple. The first test is to make sure that it is syntactically correct. This is done by running python `script.py`. This will try to execute the script using Python, and as long as the script is correct syntactically, it will execute and probably wait for some input. The next step for testing is to run a command that will pull a sample input configuration and pass it to the modular input script. All the responses from the script are presented on standard out. Here is the command (as configured for our `sdgAPI` modular input):

```
/opt/splunk/bin/splunk cmd splunkd print-modinput-config sdgAPI sdgAPI://
test | /opt/splunk/bin/splunk cmd python /opt/splunk/etc/apps/SDG/bin/
sdgAPI.py
```

The section before the pipe gets the configuration for the `sdgAPI://test` stanza, which is located in the `inputs.conf` file. The second part passes the configuration to the Python script we have written. If everything has been done correctly, the results of the API call will be output to the screen. Once you have the confirmation that the modular input will work as expected, restart Splunk. This is necessary to integrate the input into the Splunk GUI.

Configuring modular inputs

Now that we have a working modular input, we must use it. The configurations for this modular input are found in **Data Inputs** under **Settings**. After the restart, you can see a new modular input, as shown here:

sdgAPI	1	Add new
Get data from an un-authenticated REST API		

Follow these steps to configure the modular input:

1. Click on the **sdgAPI** input name and you will be taken to the input configuration manager.

2. Click on the **New** button to be taken to the parameter setup screen. You can see in the manager that the descriptions and parameter values that you set in the spec file are present and visible, as shown in this screenshot:

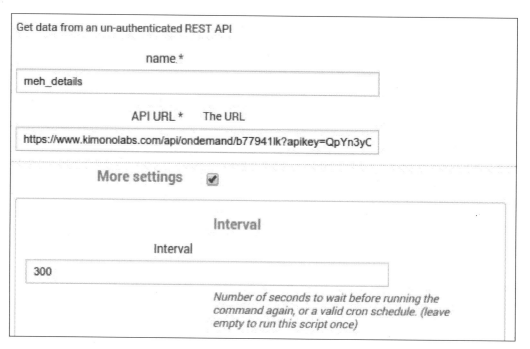

Get data from an un-authenticated REST API

name.*

meh_details

API URL *   The URL

https://www.kimonolabs.com/api/ondemand/b77941lk?apikey=QpYn3yC

More settings

Interval

Interval

300

Number of seconds to wait before running the command again, or a valid cron schedule. (leave empty to run this script once)

3. Once you have the fields filled in, click on the **Next** button, and the input is saved!

Protip

Make sure you click on **More Settings** and set your interval if you want the input to continually consume data.

You can see in the manager that the input has been saved and is enabled and active, like this:

| meh_details | https://www.kimonolabs.com/api/ondemand/b77941lk?
apikey=QpYn3yCTCAeFY7c5qqM3f754UcEWhlrd | mi_meh_details | splunk_developers_guide | Enabled \| Disable | Clone \| Delete |

And there you have it! A modular input that can be used with any non-authenticated API URL.

The App Key Value Store

The App **Key Value Store** (**KV Store**) is new in Splunk 6.2. Think of them as lookups that are stored in memory. The actual storage is done in a Mongo database that is run by the Splunk process. The KV Store is very useful for storing state data and fills a gap that existed in earlier versions of Splunk. State data is data that defines what the current condition of something is. For example, we would like to know what the most recent memory and CPU usages are for a system. You could write this data to a typical lookup file, but by using the KV Store, you can get the ability to interface with the store from within your App. The KV Store has a complete REST interface with which to perform CRUD (short for create, read, update, and delete) operations, making it invaluable and extremely flexible. You can perform these CRUD operations directly from the Splunk search language, much like a typical lookup.

When would you use the KV Store?

Well, there are quite a few instances where the KV Store is beneficial. The bigger the lookup, the slower it performs as a CSV-based lookup (up to 10 MB). So, as your lookup or state table increases, you will want to use the KV Store. The folks at http://dev.splunk.com do a *bang up* job of detailing the pros and cons of each methodology.

The pros and cons of KV Store are as follows:

Pros of the KV Store	Cons of the KV Store
Enables per-record insertions/updates (upserts)	May not work for extra large datasets (> 10 million rows)
Allows optional data type enforcement on write operations	Memory-intensive with extra large datasets
Allows you to define field accelerations to improve search performance	
Provides REST API access to the data collection	

The pros and cons of using CSV lookup are the following:

Pros of CSV	Cons of CSV
Performs well for files that are small or rarely modified	Does not provide multiuser access locking
Supports distributed search-based lookups on the index tier	Requires a full rewrite of a file for edit operations
Supports automatic lookups	Does not support REST API access

So, what actually is the KV Store? The KV Store is configured as *collections* of data. The following table illustrates database terms that you may be familiar with, with their corresponding configuration item in a KV Store:

Table	Collection
Row	Record
Column	Field
Primary key	_key
	_user

The _key field is reserved and contains a unique ID for each record. You can specify it, but if you don't, Splunk will generate one for you. The _user field is also reserved and cannot be overridden. This field contains the user ID for each record. Other than that, the KV Store is very similar to a database table. The major advantage here, however, is that the KV Store is not typically used for historical data. It could be, but that's what Splunk is for, right?

So, now let's dive into how these things work. We will start by configuring the KV Store for use with the meh.com API data. Once we have it configured, we will show you how to use it both with the Splunk search language, as well as within an HTML dashboard. Our collection will be limited to current product, poll, and forum statistics. In this way, we can quickly get the most up-to-date data without having to perform a Splunk search other than a simple lookup command.

Configuring the KV Store

The configuration of the KV Store is done entirely within the configuration files.
There is no corresponding GUI manager with which to perform the configuration.
The configurations are stored within the `collections.conf` file. Let's set up our KV
Store for the meh.com data. Edit your `collections.conf` file by adding this:

```
[meh_kv_product]
[meh_kv_forum]
[meh_kv_poll]
```

That's it! Seriously! However, this only defines the KV Store; we need to be able to
access it. Open `transforms.conf` and enter these configuration stanzas:

```
[meh_product_kv]
external_type = kvstore
collection = meh_kv_product
fields_list = _key , price, visitors, revenue, mehclicks, title
[meh_forum_kv]
external_type = kvstore
collection = meh_kv_forum
fields_list = _key , op, op_action, activity, last_activity, title,
votes
[meh_poll_kv]
external_type = kvstore
collection = meh_kv_poll
fields_list = _key , poll_id, poll_title, text, votes
```

This will configure the lookups for each of the different collections. The `fields_
list` is mandatory and defines what the lookup is allowed to interact with. This is
important because it is possible to update the KV Store via the REST interface for all
fields, while only allowing the lookup command to interact with a subset of fields.
Now that we have some place for our lookup to go, we need to populate it. To do
this, we created a macro called `product_KV_gen`.

The contents of it are as follows:

```
`meh_base` earliest=-30m@m | stats latest(deal.items{}.price) as
price latest(results.collection1{}.visitors) as visitors latest(deal.
title) as title, latest(results.collection1{}.product_total_revenue)
as revenue, latest(results.collection1{}.meh_clicks) as mehclicks |
outputlookup meh_product_kv
```

Essentially, this search is taking two different source types from the last 30 minutes and producing a table with fields that match the field list of the `meh_product` KV Store. The table should look like this:

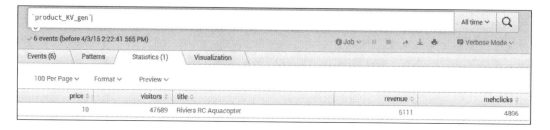

Once you have the table formatted with the same fields as the KV Store, you can use the `outputlookup` command and write the results to the KV Store. Now, this by itself won't keep the store updated. Let's save the search and run it every 5 minutes. In this way, our numbers are constantly updated as the details are updated. So now, if you want to pull the latest results, you can simply issue the `inputlookup` command on the KV lookup name, and the results are returned. We won't sit and create the other two macros and saved searches; they are done in the same way.

So now that we have this information, how do we use it? Well, you can use it in a search and display the results in the typical fashion. The other option is to interface with the REST API directly and pull and display the results as you wish. For this demonstration, we've created a new HTML dashboard that is completely blank. To create it, we have made a new SimpleXML dashboard, and then converted it to HTML. Down in the section for the SearchManager, let's add this code:

```
var APPNAME = "SDG",
        baseKV = "/servicesNS/nobody/"+APPNAME+"/
          storage/collections/data/",
        productKV = baseKV + "meh_kv_product/";
var service = mvc.createService({ owner: "nobody" });
$('#productkvlaunch').on("click", function(e){
        service.request(
                productKV,
            "GET",
            null,
            null,
            null,
            {"Content-Type": "application/json"},
            null)
                .done(function(data) {
```

```
                var myData = JSON.parse(data)[0];
                var myHTML = "<ul><li>"+myData.title+"</
li><li>Price$:"+myData.price+"</li><li>Total$:"+myData.revenue+"</
li><li>Visits:"+myData.visitors+"</li><li>Clicks:"+myData.
mehclicks+"</li></ul>";
                $('#productkvlaunch_results').html(myHTML);
            });
        });
```

Love to code! So, here's a quick breakdown. Again, this is only for one KV Store; the same method can be transferred to any other KV Store. Firstly, our variables—we use variables to help speed development and to reduce the risk of errors. If our APPNAME value changes, it will change in all the URLs configured for using it. The base URL for the KV Store is `/servicesNS/nobody/APPNAME/storage/collections/data/KVSTORENAME`, where APPNAME is, well, the App name, and KVSTORENAME is the stanza that you configured earlier in `collections.conf`. Once you have the URLs set, you need to initiate a service object. This service object can be used on pretty much any of the REST APIs, so don't limit yourself to the KV Store. Literally, any configuration option available for an endpoint is available for this service. The service is called as shown in the previous code snippet, with the arguments object passed. We are setting owner to nobody, as nobody is a special user that should have access to most configurations. Right after we create the service, we assign the `onclick` event to an HTML element (which, in our dashboard, is a header). The purpose of this is to give the user a method of interacting with the data, and we can refresh it at any point. Once into the function, we call the `request` method of the service and pass our parameters. The first is the URL of the endpoint we want; the second is the method (GET). Number six is a header object. The others can be null for this request. The last step is to do something with the results once the request returns, so we tack a `.done` function and pass the data that was returned. In this case, the `done` function prints the returned data on the console. The data returned is a string and looks like this:

```
[ { "mehclicks" : "4930", "price" : "10", "revenue" : "5111",
  "title" : "Riviera RC Aquacopter", "visitors" : "50739", "_user"
  : "nobody", "_key" : "551eeee9911c2730cd6ca6a1" } ]
```

To use this string as an object, use the JSON features of JavaScript and convert it to `.json` objects. From this object, you are now free to move about the cabin, er... the dashboard. You can update a D3 visualization, or simply build an unordered list with the results. Here, we built an unordered list and updated the inside of another element. The options are boundless and are limited only by your imagination. While this is only a read example of CRUD, you can perform any of the other operations using the `service.request` function and pass the needed values. The complete documentation is available online at `http://dev.splunk.com`.

Data models

Data models are becoming an essential part of the App developer's toolkit. They help developers design and maintain the *semantic knowledge* of their data. Semantic knowledge can be described as the underlying knowledge of the meaning and assessment of the data that is being consumed. This knowledge is typically known only to subject matter experts, but it can be transferred to the end user in the form of data models. These data models can then be summarized and accelerated as needed with Splunk Enterprise. Data models are also the driving force behind the **Pivot** feature of Splunk Enterprise. They define how data is related and/or broken down. They are created using searches that are *tiered* into different sections. For example, your root event may be `tag=web_logs` (which says that you want all web logs, including IIS or Apache), and the second tier may be `Errors`, which will constrain the *child search* to only web log errors (for example, `status = 500`). This gives the end user the ability to choose the web log errors and then use Pivot to drill down to any remaining attributes (also known as *fields*).

A data model starts with one or more objects. Here is a quick list of facts about these objects that can be found at `http://docs.splunk.com/Documentation/Splunk`:

- An object is a specification for a dataset. Each data model object corresponds in some manner to a set of data in an index. You can apply data models to different indexes and get different datasets.

- Objects can be broken down into four types: event objects, search objects, transaction objects, and child objects.

- Objects are hierarchical. Objects in data models can be arranged hierarchically in parent-child relationships. The top-level event, search, and transaction objects in data models are collectively referred to as **root objects**.

- Child objects have inheritance. Data model objects are defined by characteristics that mostly break down into constraints and attributes. Child objects inherit constraints and attributes from their parent objects and have additional constraints and attributes of their own.

The first object defined in a data model is called the root object. There can be more than one root object, and each can be of a different type. The three types are **event**, **transaction**, and **search**. Let's take a quick look at each of them.

The first type of object is the root event. These objects are the most commonly used by developers. Each event object represents a type of event, very similar to the event type configurations in Splunk, as we saw in *Chapter 3, Enhancing Applications*. Root event objects are defined using simple constraints, which are basically the first part of a typical search, before any other search command.

The second type of object is the root transaction. These give the developer the ability to create *transactions* across a subset of data. A transaction is defined as a related group of events that cross time. Before you can create a root transaction object, you must have either an event or a search root object defined in the data model.

The last type of object is the root search. This object can be almost any Splunk search, including other commands. This gives you the ability to transform events and fields within the data model, which can then be further constrained by child objects.

 Child objects of each root type are defined with a *simple constraint*. These constraints narrow down the data from the parent objects.

Data models can be accelerated, making them perfect for use within an App for performance reasons. However, only root event objects can be accelerated. If you have a very large transforming search, you will most likely want to find the equivalent simple constraint search for use with acceleration.

Object constraints (used with each type of data model object) help filter events into a *schema* or *dataset*. A root event object will have a *simple search* as its constraint, which means that there are no transforming or streaming commands in the search string. A root search object uses the base search string and can include transformations within the string. A root transaction object is constrained by the transaction definition. These definitions must identify group objects and one or more *group by* fields. This is similar in configuration and usage to the transaction command used in the search bar.

Each object also has object attributes. These are essentially *fields* that have been extracted or presented in some way. There are five different types of attributes found at `http://docs.splunk.com/Documentation/Splunk`, which are as follows:

- **Auto-extracted**: This is a field that Splunk Enterprise derives at search time. You can add auto-extracted attributes to root objects only. Child objects can only inherit them, and they cannot add new auto-extracted attributes of their own. Auto-extracted attributes can be any of the following:
    - Fields that Splunk Enterprise recognizes and extracts automatically, such as `uri` or `version`. This includes fields indexed through structured data inputs, such as fields extracted from the headers of indexed CSV files.
    - Field extractions, lookups, or calculated fields that you have defined in **Settings** or configured in `inprops.conf`.

○ Fields that you have manually added to the attribute because they aren't currently in the object dataset, but should be in the future. This can include fields that are added to the object dataset by generating commands such as `inputcsv` or `dbinspect`.

- **Eval expression**: This is a field derived from an eval expression that you enter in the attribute definition. Eval expressions often involve one or more extracted fields.

- **Lookup**: This is a field that is added to the events in the object dataset with the help of a lookup that you configure in the attribute definition. Lookups add fields from external data sources, such as CSV files and scripts. When you define a lookup attribute, you can use any lookup that you have defined in **Settings** and associate it with any other attribute that has already been associated with the same object.

- **Regular expression**: This attribute type represents a field that is extracted from the object event data using a regular expression that you provide in the attribute definition. A regular expression attribute definition can use a regular expression that extracts multiple fields. Each field will appear in the object attribute list as a separate regular expression attribute.

- **Geo IP**: This is a specific type of lookup that adds geographical attributes, such as latitude, longitude, country, and city, to events in the object dataset that have valid IP address fields. It is useful for map-related visualizations.

Attributes can be inherited, extracted, or calculated. Inherited attributes *drop through* different objects. Child attributes inherit attributes from the parent object, making it necessary for each parent to have the attributes required by each child. Extracted attributes are those that are auto-extracted from the search results. Finally, calculated attributes are configured through calculation or lookup within the data model.

Data models can be quite complex or they can be really simple. The extensibility of a data model gives you flexibility to define your data and present it to the end user as a *structured schema* based on unstructured data. You can create and manage data models on the management page, found in **Data Models** under **Settings**. Let's navigate there now, so we can create a simple one, just to get an idea of what's going on.

Once you are at the **Data Models** manager, click on **Create New**. This will load a quick form to enter your data model name, as shown in the following screenshot:

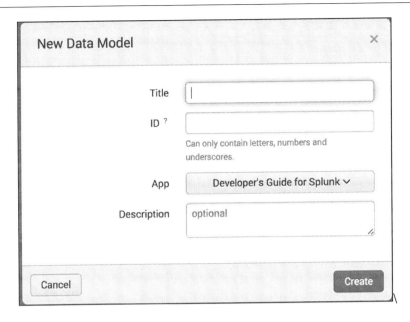

Once you have created the base data model, you need to add objects, as we discussed earlier in the chapter. You can do this by using the drop-down menu and then choosing your root item:

Then, it's as simple as filling in the items that are required and choosing the fields you want to add into that object:

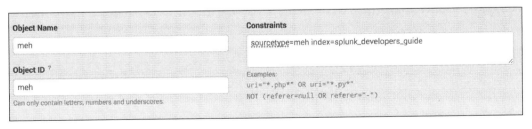

This will be the base of the data model. You can put literally any search here that you want to use as long as it is a base search only. Any other search commands cannot be placed here. Once you have your events, choose your fields!

It's that simple! Once you have built the root objects, add the child objects. The child objects are just more searches that narrow down the scope of the data model. A child object may then look like this:

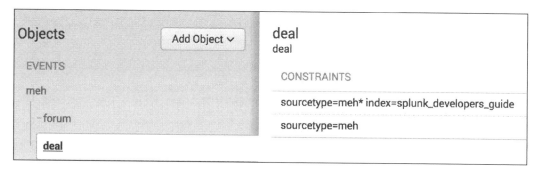

As you can see, data models can help you narrow down large datasets into more manageable chunks, which then can be used in searches. Accelerate a data model, and you've got a fast and easy way of referencing large datasets.

Version control and package managers

Version control is fairly important in the realm of a Splunk App. When publishing your Apps, you must include version numbers, and the easiest way to keep a track of the changes is with version control. We will focus on Git, as it is a standard of version control. You can just as easily use CVS or SVN, but Git is much more flexible and easier to work with. Since almost everything in a Splunk App is ASCII-based (very few and far binary files), Apps are more easily integrated with version control systems. Package managers are a newer concept, at least in the realm of web development.

The two we will cover (npm and Bower) are specifically designed for web applications, and a lot of hard work in finding, updating, and converting JavaScript libraries has already been done for you. Gulp is another tool we will investigate. It is a streaming build system that can automatically watch files for changes, update static library contents, and provide minification for your JavaScript. Each of these tools was selected by how well it meshes with the Splunk architecture and design. You can use other tools, but these are popular, robust, and extensible.

You may ask yourself: Why should I bother about a package manager? Well, it can be said that the ability to publish an App, with the ability to be updated on the fly, is a great feature. For example, most themed Apps will include all the themes a user might wish to use, but never uses. This wastes space on the filesystems, in the cloud, and over the wire. Using a package manager, you can include the configuration for a specific theming library, and provide the user with instructions on how to get the theme they want. We'll cover this in more depth in just a little while; for now, let's start with npm.

npm

The Node Package Manager (`https://www.npmjs.com`) allows developers to share reusable code and provides an easy way to update that shared code. Most of the packages available through npm are specifically for Node.js, which is a platform built on JavaScript, designed to build fast and scalable network applications. While most of these packages don't work directly with the Splunk Web Framework, we can take advantage of the other tool packages available. Bower and Gulp are both npm packages and can be downloaded as such. Configurations for npm are normally contained within the `package.json` file. In our case, we will store this file in `appserver/static/build`. This gives us a work area in which to put modules and libraries, which we can then exclude from the final build when we go for publishing. This program must be installed using your OS package manager or via download links available at its website.

Bower

Bower (`http://bower.io`) is a package manager for the Web. D3, AngularJS, Bootstrap, Font Awesome, and jQuery are just a few of the libraries you can manage with Bower. D3 and jQuery fit right into the work we've been doing with the Splunk Web Framework. Configurations for Bower are contained in the `bower.json` file, which we will also place in the `appserver/static/build` folder. We will add each of the libraries we need to this file, along with specific version information, if needed. Bower is installed using npm and by including it in the `package.json` configuration file.

Gulp

Gulp (http://gulpjs.com) is a streaming build system. With many modular plugins, Gulp is very flexible as per your needs. It is very good at compiling static content into a single file. This gives you the ability to build a multitude of CSS files into a single application.css file. Why? Because you don't have to touch every dashboard to include the new CSS files. Build it to one file and include just that file. It's cacheable and *accelerate-able*, and doesn't have to be polled multiple times. You can do the same thing for images or JavaScript files. The default file for configuring Gulp is gulpfile.js, which we will place in the appserver/static/build folder. Gulp is another npm module and is installed in the same way as Bower. Each Gulp plugin needs to be installed via npm as well, but once you see how easy it is, you won't want to do it any other way!

Git

Git (http://git-scm.com) is a distributed version control system that works very well with ASCII text projects (such as Splunk Apps). It is not a module of npm. Rather, it must be installed as a package on your OS of choice. It is lightweight, open source, and free. There is no direct configuration file for Git as there is for the other tools. You will have to initialize a repository in the base of your App and add files and other items that you want to keep a track of in the repository. Keeping your App under version control helps you keep a track of changes between releases, and in case anything gets deleted accidentally (as long as it was under version control in the first place). Git even offers the ability to push your changes to an external repository (such as GitHub), where others can download, fork, or ask for a pull request (a code merge).

Tying them all together

Now that you know what tools you want to use, let's put them into practice to replace the bits of our App. Let's start by defining what tools we want to install with npm. We are going to use our appserver/static/build folder; we will do this with npm. Firstly, you will need to install npm on your operating system. Instructions are available at npm's website. In the package.json file, add this content:

```
{
    "name": "SDG",
    "version": "0.0.1",
    "author": "alacercogitatus",
    "devDependencies": {
```

```
    "bower": "latest",
    "gulp": "~3.8.6",
    "gulp-bower": "0.0.6",
    "gulp-concat": "~2.3.3",
    "gulp-less":"latest"
  }
}
```

This is exactly how yours needs to be typed out. It should be in a pure JSON string, not just a JavaScript literal object. The name attribute is the name of your App, as best practice. Typically, name is the name of the npm module, but since we aren't packaging this for publishing to npm, we can use our App name. Add your App version and author, as shown in the following code snippet. The real magic is in the devDependencies section. In here, you list which tools you need to grab via npm and their version number.

Specifying latest will get you the—ta da!—latest version! Now that we have a configuration file, we execute the npm install command (in the same folder as the file). This will download, compile, and install the npm modules, making them available for you to use. You will notice that there is a new folder, node_modules, which contains the modules you just downloaded for use. We now have Bower and Gulp at our disposal for building the rest of the App.

Let's start with Bower, since it will give us the basic libraries we need. The libraries we want to include are **d3** and the **sidr** jQuery plugin. The first step is to visit Bower's website and find the appropriate package name. In this case, we want to use the d3 and sidr packages. Let's add this code to the bower.json file we have in the build folder:

```
{
  "name": "SDG",
  "version": "0.0.1",
  "authors": [
    "alacercogitatus"
  ],
  "description": "Splunk Developer's Guide Bower",
  "dependencies": {
    "d3": "latest",
    "sidr" : "latest"
  }
}
```

This file should also be a pure JSON object, not just a JavaScript object literal. In a style similar to that of the `package.json` file, we place the packages we require in the `dependencies` object, with the version that we require. Once the file is saved, you have to run `bower install`. This command will read the Bower configuration file and download the libraries in a new folder, `bower_components`. In this folder, you will find all the JavaScript files necessary for using d3 and sidr. They are in the same form as they would be if you had downloaded them from the Internet. Next up—Gulp!

Gulp is a streaming build system that is designed to compile and distribute just about anything where it needs to go. The configurations are based in the `gulpfile.js` file. Let's populate our file:

```javascript
var gulp = require('gulp'),
        bower = require('gulp-bower'),
        concat = require('gulp-concat'),
        less = require('gulp-less'),
        rename = require('gulp-rename');

gulp.task('copy:requires', function(){
        gulp.src([
                './bower_components/d3/d3.min.js',
                './bower_components/sidr/jquery.sidr.min.js'
                ])
                .pipe(rename(function(path) {path["dirname"] =
                  "";}))
                .pipe(gulp.dest('../js'));
});

gulp.task('default',[ 'copy:requires'], function() {});
```

This file is a little more complicated than the other configuration files. It needs to be written in JavaScript. At the very top of the file, set the variables that are assigned by requiring the npm modules that were defined in the `package.json` file. These variables will be referenced later in the file as functions. Gulp uses definitions called *tasks* to perform functions. In our case, we have created a `copy:requires` task, which takes the two libraries we need and copies them to the `appserver/static/js` folder. This task is referenced by the `default` task so that every time Gulp is executed without a task being specified, the `default` task is executed. There are many other tasks that can be performed with Gulp and many more plugins. Once you have the file in place and configured, simply run `gulp`. The files will be copied to the correct location. By combining these three tools, you can package an App to have the ability to be updated to the latest package versions of web frameworks and other tools, as well as enforce specific versions as needed. You can even include a build script that executes each tool—one right after another—to automate the process.

Now let's set up Git. Git will help us keep a track of what we changed and give us an opportunity to keep track of versions with tags. It has the ability to push changes to a remote repository to share or just keep as an offsite backup. It is installed on the operating system just like npm. Once it is installed, navigate to the root folder of your App. Issue these commands:

1. `git init`
2. `git add`
3. `git commit -am ' Initial Commit'`

These commands initialize the repository, add all the files to it, and finally commit the changes made to it. That's it! It's simple to use, and helps keep a track of changes made to your App. As you add new files and make changes to existing ones, you have to issue commands 2 and 3 from the preceding list respectively. This ensures that your changes are up to date and saved in the repository.

> **Protip**
> If you employ using the `build` folder, you will definitely want to add the following code to the `.gitignore` file. This will tell Git to ignore the downloaded files so that they are not added to your repository. This keeps the repository light and ready for packaging and publishing.

Add this configuration to the `.gitignore` file in the `appserver/static/build` folder to ignore the directories:

```
node_modules
bower_components
!./package.json
!./bower.json
!./gulpfile.js
```

There are many more things you can do with Git; this is just a basic introduction to version control. To find out more, visit the Git website (`http://git-scm.com`).

Summary

In this chapter, we converted an inline visualization into a customized SimpleSplunkView. As we saw, the benefits of this conversion are incredible. The modular ability allows the same code to be used over and over, without the likelihood of making mistakes in the copy-and-paste process. Once you've included the JavaScript in the base RequireJS stack, you can take advantage of the objects and instantiate the objects wherever you like.

After JavaScript views, we dove into modular inputs. Modular inputs give us the ability to reuse a script, while providing the end user with a simple interface with which to do the configuration as required. They can also be configured to take advantage of encrypted credentials within the script, securing your credentials from the casual observer. We discussed portions of the script and how they relate to the total implementation.

We discussed the KV Store and the benefits of using it versus file-based lookups. We explored how to create them and how to interact with them. Using KV Stores is very beneficial when creating state tables, as well as when the full gambit of CRUD operations is desired. We then showed you how to integrate a KV Store into an HTML dashboard using the REST API and the JavaScript service object.

We then went over some tools designed to help keep your App configurable and shareable. Using tools such as package managers and version control, you can share an App with a team and ensure that everybody is using the same version of libraries and code. This is done to minimize code problems. Version control is especially helpful, and Splunk Apps lend themselves well to it.

In the next chapter, we will discuss how to package your App for other users to use and install.

7
Packaging Applications

In this chapter, we will cover how to properly package your App for publishing. Packaging your App correctly is critical to allowing you to publish the App on **Splunkbase**. Splunk provides a set of guidelines and standards that must be met for your App to be included on Splunkbase. Splunkbase is the official repository for Splunk Apps and add-ons, created by both Splunk and other contributors. Packaging also gives you the opportunity to brand and document your App in a manner that clearly defines you and your brand. Splunkbase automatically checks the structure of your App when you upload it, so it is important to make sure you cross your Ts and dot your Is before you upload. As we progress through this chapter, we will package our App and get it ready for deployment to Splunkbase. We will first go over the naming guidelines, and then cover some standards and best practices. Once we detail what needs to happen, we will see how to actually package the App.

Naming guidelines

Splunk has provided a very nice set of guidelines for use in packaging your App. These guidelines are important, as you do not want to infringe on any copyrights or licensed trademarks as you build your App.

These are *guidelines*, and while your App can literally be named anything you want for use, either internally in a company or for an individual install, you *must* follow the guidelines to publish on Splunkbase.

The first guideline revolves around using third-party trademarks. A third-party trademark is anything that you or Splunk do not own, control, or have license to use except under fair use. When using a third party trademark, Splunk maintains that you must separate the third party's trademark from the Splunk trademark with the word *for*, which:

- Clarifies that the third-party trademark and associated technology do not belong to Splunk or the author of the App or add-on.

- Indicates that the App or add-on works with a specific third-party product. You should include the technology name for the third-party product, although you can drop the technology where the trademark could only be referring to only one product.

For example, *Nagios for Splunk* is a valid App name, whereas *Splunk App for Nagios* is not. You should take care to make sure you are naming your App correctly, as you don't want to confuse the users or infringe on trademarks. Along these lines, do not use a third-party logo, unless you are licensed to do so. Certain companies allow you to use their logos under specific guidelines, and you should check their guidelines to make sure you are compliant with them. Never use the ® symbol when describing your App, or in your App name, as it pertains to a third party. There are guidelines for using a third-party trademark in your App name, but there are also guidelines that govern the name of an App that a non-Splunk party has built (meaning you). If you reference Splunk's registered trademarks in any of your documentations, web presence, or headers, you must use the ® symbol next to Splunk's name. Make sure that your App doesn't imply that Splunk built or includes your App in the product. Also you may not have a press conference relating to the release of your App, unless you are a formal partner and adhere to the Splunk press release guidelines.

Another part of packaging is making sure that you will meet the approval criteria for Splunkbase, which are essentially standards to keep the community vibrant and trustworthy. Let's run a list of standards and additional naming conventions required to start the packaging process.

- **App ID**: The ID attribute for the App must be filled out in `app.conf`. This ID should be unique so that when installed, the ID is unique from any other App on the instance. It can simply be the name of the folder.

- **App version**: The `version` attribute must have a string defined. Normal versioning methods can be used (major, minor, maintenance, and so on).

- **App description**: This needs to be short and sweet. Keep it informative, yet concise.

- **App icons and screenshots**: Icons that are displayed on Splunkbase are pulled from the `appserver/static` directory in your App. They are required to be in PNG format and 36px x 36px resolution. Screenshots are also shown on Splunkbase, and must be in PNG format and 623px x 350px resolution.

Let's review our `app.conf` file and make sure that we have everything we need to package the App:

```
[install]
is_configured = 0
[ui]
is_visible = 1
label = Developer's Guide for Splunk
[launcher]
author = Kyle Smith
description = Developer's Guide Example for Splunk
version = 1.0
[package]
id = SDG
```

Yep, we have the requirements for the `app.conf` file. All the required options are filled in (version, description, and ID), and we're ready to go.

> The App ID *must* match the name of the folder in which your App lives. Once this is uploaded to Splunkbase, it *cannot* be changed, and a new App will need to be uploaded if the ID does need change.

Do you remember the icon we created earlier? We copied that to the `appserver/static` folder to make sure it gets displayed on Splunkbase. Any source code you have in your App must also meet certain standards, and will be peer reviewed by Splunk. If you have any binary content, it should be what it is supposed to be (in other words, don't end a file with `.exe` if it is a `.png` file). Any executable files must be located in the `bin` folder of your App. Operating system considerations must also meet standards. If you have a script that says it is executable, make sure it is executable. Don't add any malicious commands such as `rm -rf` or `kill -9` and the like. These are some of the standards used when evaluating your App. Follow these and your App should be approved; most of them are common sense (like don't execute `rm -rf` — for *real*, don't do it.) The list is ever-evolving; you can find the most up-to-date version at `http://docs.splunk.com/Documentation/Splunkbase/latest/Splunkbase/Approvalcriteria`.

Dos and don'ts

Let's review a quick table of some dos and don'ts when it comes to App packaging. This table might give you some ideas of other configurations you may want to include, but it is by no means exhaustive:

Don'ts	Dos
Hard code index names into searches and dashboards.	Use macros and event types to allow end user customization of index locations.
Leave compiled Python code files in any folder.	Remove the `*.pyc` files.
Leave anything in the `local` folder.	Move it all to the `default` folder.
Use odd or obtuse naming of fields in extractions.	Make use of the Splunk Common Information Model.
Allow users to edit source code to add configurations.	Use a setup file or modular input to allow user configurations.
Include no logging, or use obtuse abbreviations.	Log in `key=value` with descriptive information.
Use hardcoded paths or OS-specific options.	Use Python libraries to build paths and environment.
Leave unused libraries and frameworks in `bin`.	Use Bower, npm, Gulp, and Git to keep the build clean.
Leave inputs enabled by default.	Allow users to choose what to enable.
Include an index configuration.	"Test, test, and test"
	Include a screenshot and icon. Brand recognition is everything.
Leave hidden files in any folder (you see, OS X users).	Follow the published guidelines.

The reason you should not include an index configuration is not always clear. An App should not dictate where in the environment the data should be placed; that is up to the Splunk administrator. If you place a default configuration for the index, you could possibly cause disk space issues if the default location is not designed for the data.

Packaging the App

Now we actually get to package the App in preparation for publishing. We will cover how to use both a *nix command line as well as 7-Zip for Windows. We will carry out the compression only after readying the folder structure for packaging. Let's start by copying the entire App folder to a new location. This makes sure that we get a clean directory to move files and content within. If you are using Git, you can also simply commit the dev changes and clone the repository into a different folder. This is beneficial, since earlier we had some build files in the `appserver/static` folder, but they didn't make it into the repository. Keep it clean, and keep it small!

Once you have relocated your App, we can start with the actual packaging. The first thing to remove is the `metadata/local.meta` file. The next thing is to check the default permissions in `metadata/default.meta`. If they look good, let's move on to the `bin` folder. This is where you would want to remove any `*.pyc` files, as they need to be compiled on the target system. Next, check your `appserver/static` folder to make sure that frameworks and libraries are removed. We used Git, so our `build` folder only contains `bower.json`, `gulpfile.js`, and `package.json`. Nice and neat! Easy cleanup! However, if needed, the sources can be quickly brought in. Next, we clean up the `lookups` folder, unless it is a static lookup. Dynamic lookups need to be generated on the end user's system, so we need to remove our development copy. Now we'll move on to the harder part of packaging: combining the `default` and `local` folders.

There a few ways to approach combining the folders. The first, and least technical, approach is using a text editor to copy and paste the stanzas from `local` back to `default` for each configuration file, and then copy the files located in the `data` folder one by one. This is prone to human error (you may miss something, or paste it wrong).

Another approach is to use the Splunk Btool to generate your configuration files. Btool is a Splunk-specific command that merges the configurations into a single output, based on the file precedence rules. The following is a bash script (for use on *nix systems) that cycles through all of the local configuration files in your App, presents the merged configuration, and writes the configuration to a local folder within the `bin` folder. There, you can verify the output, and copy them over to the `default` folder. Once copied, delete the local configuration files:

```bash
#!/bin/bash
CONFS=();
for entry in ../local/*.conf
do
  myPath=${entry##*/}
```

```
    filename=${myPath%.*conf}
    if [ -f "$entry" ];then
      CONFS=("${CONFS[@]}""$filename")
    fi
done
echo ${CONFS[@]}
for conf in ${CONFS[@]}; do
  echo "Writing to $conf.conf"
  /opt/splunk/bin/splunk cmd btool $conf list --app=$1 > ./
mergedConfs/$conf.conf
done
echo "Files written into mergedConfs. Copy where desired!"
```

This is very useful, mainly because it can mitigate the copy-paste errors, since the configuration is how Splunk sees it. It is placed in the `bin` folder, and executed like this: `./package.sh SDG`. Here, `SDG` is the name of your App.

If you are going to use this script, make sure *all* of your configurations have the App-level permissions assigned to them, and are in the App scope for your App, before running the command.

Once you are done verifying the changes and have completed the move from `local` to `default`, you can move the local data files over. These are files located at `local/data`. These are not merged; they overwrite the default files. Simply copy them from their location in `local/data` to the correct location at `default/data`.

Once you have moved everything around and deleted the `local` folder, you are ready for compression. Let's do this in *nix first, and then Windows. Navigate to the parent directory of your App location and then run these commands:

- `tar -cvf SDG.tar SDG`
- `gzip SDG.tar`
- `mv SDG.tar.gz SDG.spl`

These commands create the properly named App tarball, for use with Splunk. Notice the `.spl` extension; that is how we know it is a Splunk App, and it will be handled accordingly. Unfortunately, it is not as easy on Windows. For Windows, we have to use 7-Zip, which is available at `http://www.7-zip.org/`. For this, again, navigate to the parent folder of the App. Once 7-Zip is installed, you will be able to gain right-click access to the software. Right-click on the `App` folder; you will see the following options:

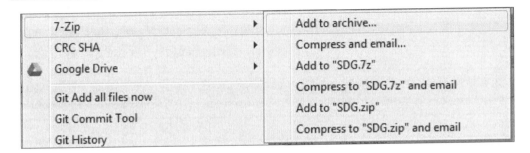

Open up the **Add to archive...** dialog, which looks like this:

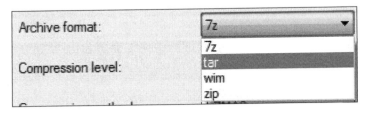

Make sure you select **tar** as the archive, since that is a requirement for the SPL file. Once you have a tar file, you need to compress it. Right-click on it again and select **Add to archive...**, but this time, select **gzip** and click on **OK**. This will compress the tar file, creating a `tar.gz` file:

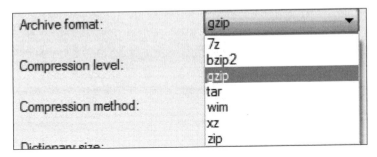

After compression, the only thing left to do is rename the file to the correct extension, `.spl`:

There is another method of packaging the App from the command line. Simply execute the following command and the App will be packaged for distribution. The command will output the location of the final package. While this is a quick method for packaging Apps, take care of its use. It does not automatically clean unused code, check for proper execution in scripts, or remove unnecessary configurations. If you are planning to distribute the package via Splunkbase, we recommend using a build system or scripts to make sure that you clean up unnecessary items.

```
$SPLUNK_HOME/bin/splunk package app <folder_name>
```

And that's it! Now you have a properly packaged Splunk App. From here, we'll move on to publishing the App using Splunkbase or your own internal service.

The App packaging checklist

The App packing checklist table is a non-all-inclusive checklist for App packaging requirements. Not every item on this list needs to be in every App, but it should provide a basic reminder of what is required:

Basic checklist		
Basic README file	XML is well formed	Empty `local` directory
Contact information	App description	Delete metadata/`local.meta`
Clean of viruses/malware	App ID	Verify default permissions
No malicious commands	App version	Remove dynamic lookups
Executables located in `bin`	App icon	No hardcoded paths
SPL file format	Common Information Model compliance	Setup screen
App name complies with guidelines	Valid EULA	No hardcoded index paths

Summary

In this chapter, we covered the Splunk guidelines for naming conventions. Naming your App incorrectly could cause an infringement of intellectual property. Make sure you use third-party trademarks properly, following both Splunk's and the third party's guidelines. We covered the basic options needed for the app.conf file, and went through the standards for content located within the App. We saw how to combine the configurations and how to finalize the package, making it ready for publishing.

We went through a list of dos and don'ts of things to do within an App, and provided an App checklist as a reminder of what is required and what you need to make sure is presented within the App. While these lists are not exhaustive, they provide a basic measure to test your Apps against.

In our final chapter, we will cover how to publish the App to Splunkbase, as well as some other areas where you can receive support from the Splunk community.

8

Publishing Applications

In this chapter, we will cover how to publish our App on Splunkbase, the community for Splunk developers. We will discuss the process step by step, and any caveats that may arise. We will talk about Certified Applications, and what that means to you as an App developer. We will also start a discussion on communities, and why the community is important in the culture of Splunk, as well as around the globe.

Then we will see some links and references to other commonly used Splunk resources, such as the Splunk Wiki and the Splunk documentation (which you should already be familiar with). Finally, we will hit upon Splunk user groups, how to find a group, and what to expect.

Self-hosting your App

The first method of publishing an App is by doing it yourself. This can mean that you are storing the data, keeping the App under control, and generally excluding Splunkbase altogether. This is a good methodology, especially when you are trying to monetize your App on a per-license basis. Splunkbase doesn't have a methodology for restricting downloads, other than for export reasons. Really, if you don't use Splunkbase, you can publish your App anywhere, and as long as people find it and download it, it is published. There are many different ways to share your App. These are just a few: Apache/IIS web server, Amazon S3, and Dropbox. It's a short list, not meant to be comprehensive, but just enough to give you ideas on where to publish and display your App.

Splunkbase

The primary location for hosted Apps is `http://apps.splunk.com`, more commonly known as Splunkbase. Splunkbase is a place for developers to publish their work under a set of various licenses and hosting options. Once you have packaged your App successfully, head over to `http://apps.splunk.com/new` and log in to your account. There will be an EULA and a privacy policy. Read and accept both of them if you agree to the terms. The first step is to determine how you are hosting your content. There are two ways of doing this: Splunk-hosted content and externally hosted content. The externally hosted option allows you to specify a URL for the end user. It contains the App and any other documentation you wish to include. This is what the option looks like:

	Hosted on Splunkbase	Hosted Externally
External Site URL		
Link to your own app website. ☑ Learn more		
http://www.company.com/app		

The other option is to have it hosted by Splunkbase. This option will look like this:

Hosted on Splunkbase	Hosted Externally
Drop package here or Choose file	
Extension must be tar.gz or zip; Max size 50 MB; Max 1 file	
📄 SDG.spl	

If your browser supports it, you will have the option of a file picker or drag and drop. Notice the requirements: maximum size of 50 MB and only one file at a time. The extension must be `tar.gz`, `.zip`, or `.spl` (although `.spl` is not currently listed). As soon as you upload the package, Splunkbase validates the App and informs you of any validation errors.

Any errors during the next steps will be presented at the top of the page, and will look like this:

> ⚠ Name can only contain alphanumeric characters or +,-,.,!,/,\

Here, the error was a special character in the name of the App. Also, on the initial upload page, there is additional metadata that should be filled in to help users filter down to your App as it applies to them:

Splunk Version
☐ 6.2 ☐ 6.1 ☐ 6.0 ☐ 5.0

Deployment Types
☐ Single Search Head ☑ Distributed

App Contents
☑ Dashboards ☐ Inputs ☑ Sourcetypes ☐ TAs

CIM
☐ 4.1 ☐ 4.0 ☐ 3.0

 Make sure that whatever boxes you check actually apply to your environment. This is important if you are going to request App certification.

We'll define App certification in a moment. As you step through the web UI, fill in the relevant details for your App. Make them as complete as possible, especially sections that are used for documentation. Take careful note of the **License** page. You can specify a *Free as in Beer* license, but you can also restrict it to any number of different types of licenses. You can even charge fees for your App. You can find out more about the different licenses, and which of them you may want to use, at `http://choosealicense.com/`.

Once you have stepped through the wizard and all configurations have been initially validated, your App will be placed in a *holding pattern*, there to remain until a Splunk employee reviews it, based on the approval criteria we discussed earlier. You can view your App and make changes to the metadata but, until it has been approved, no one will be able to see it.

Your App may look something like this:

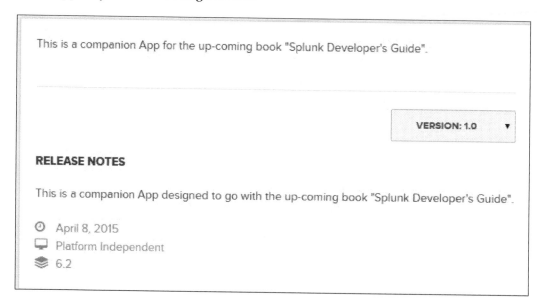

Of course, you will want to make the release notes and description more meaningful, but very quickly, you can see some basic information about your App. And that's it as far as uploading and publishing your App on Splunkbase is concerned! Quick and easy! However, if you want to learn more about Certified Applications, read on.

Certified Applications

Certified Applications is a program provided by Splunk. These Certified Applications programs are inspected and examined by the awesome people at Splunk. Both Apps and add-ons are eligible for certification. The source code is evaluated for vulnerabilities and, in essence, Splunk is committed to back the quality and status of the App or add-on. Many customers who may be downloading your App might have concerns with the security of the App. Make sure to take the time and test and evaluate your code for vulnerabilities and coding best practices. Take special consideration when considering the following excerpt, which can be found at http://docs.splunk.com/Documentation:

> "*Splunk does not, in any way, warrant the accuracy, reliability, completeness, usefulness, non-infringement of our community or partner developers. Splunk shall not be liable or responsible in any way for any losses or damage of any kind including lost profits or other indirect or consequential damages related to the use or, or reliance upon, Splunk certified apps or add-ons.*"

There are certain benefits of this for developers and users. Users get the assurance that an App or add-on has been peer reviewed and it executes with the highest standards without harming their systems and data. They also get that warm and fuzzy feeling knowing that a certified App will have the proper support that most enterprises expect. While the SLA for each App will be different, there should be a minimum level of support offered as a certification requirement. This requirement is part of the certification requirements, which are listed later. For developers, certification means a prominent place on Splunkbase and more visibility, with the recognition that the App or add-on was designed and executed beautifully. The really awesome benefit for developers is the ability to access prerelease builds of Splunk Enterprise (with a valid nondisclosure agreement). This gives you the ability to refactor and release new builds with each new Splunk release.

The list of requirements for certification is pretty long. We won't hit every point, as the requirements may change, but the primary requirements are these:

- Dependency declarations
- Index creation
- Summarization and acceleration techniques
- CIM support
- Eventgen support (required with CIM support)
- Documentation
- Support

There are also recommended criteria that go deeper down the Splunk rabbit hole, as well as a nifty checklist for certification. You can find the nitty-gritty right here at `http://dev.splunk.com/view/app-cert/SP-CAAAE3H`.

 The support requirement details that you must have 8-hour x 5-day support available. Make sure that you can commit to this requirement.

As part of the certification process, you need to follow the security best practices guidelines. Some of these guidelines are essential for all types of IT-related projects, such as keeping track of security in your software life cycle, following the **Open Web Application Security Project** (**OWASP**) site and practices, ensuring that third-party content is up to date and secure, and manually testing every portion with the controls listed at OWASP.

The certification process is pretty simple! Start by building an App, which we hopefully helped you accomplish. Next, double and triple check the criteria against your App and then package it. Before requesting certification, make sure that you provide documentation and support information in the App or add-on. One of the biggest reasons for failing in certification is not documenting thoroughly enough. Once you feel you have met the criteria, you can submit your App to Splunkbase normally, but make sure that you check the **Certification** box. This triggers the review process and, when approved, you will have published a certified App!

Splunk Cloud applications

Recently, Splunk started offering an in-cloud hosted version of Splunk. This offering is different in a few ways, which will impact your choices for deploying Apps into Splunk Cloud. Apps cannot be installed directly into Splunk Cloud by the end user. Splunk must vet each App prior to installation. Splunk support can help you install an App into Splunk Cloud. As you are developing Apps, you should keep these points in mind:

- Splunk-supported Apps are available in Splunk Cloud.
- Community Apps and custom Apps are allowed in Splunk Cloud after a vetting process by the Splunk Cloud team.
- Apps with certain features such as scripted inputs or third-party credentials must be run on a heavy forwarder that you manage on premises. The heavy forwarder sends the parsed data to Splunk Cloud.

While you might not have direct control in the environment, keep in mind that a customer might want your App in Splunk Cloud. Design it now, save time and hassle later.

Community

Now that we have uploaded our App, we can truthfully say we have joined the Splunk community. Also, as part of the Splunk community, we have certain responsibilities to foster the environment as an inviting place to explore, learn, and help others. We will now take a moment to orient those of you that haven't yet visited the community.

Answers

The answers site is a help forum that is open to the public. It is located at `http://answers.splunk.com`. The primary purpose is to get help from other forum members. The questions that are asked and the answers that are given are highly variable, but the amount of creativity is astounding. Most of these answers come from folks with a wealth of real-world knowledge, but some are answered by native Splunkers. No question is too small; the community is always willing to help.

dev.splunk.com

As the title indicates, `http://dev.splunk.com` is a site designed for App developers, and almost everything in this book can be found in the documentation there. The site covers the HTML web framework, as well as the Django environment (deprecated in 6.3) and an entire list of SDKs—definitely a site to use for your reference.

Internet Relay Chat

Internet Relay Chat (IRC) has been around for a very long time. If you are interested in the multiplayer notepad, join us at the #splunk IRC Channel on EFnet. There are various IRC clients that can be used; most of them use Adium, Irssi, and others. If you need help connecting to IRC, check out `http://wiki.splunk.com/Community:IRC`.

Wiki

A Wiki is a place meant to gather information; Splunk has one. It is full of information, and is located at `http://wiki.splunk.com`. There are quite a few things posted on the Wiki—too many to mention all of them—but there are a few gems that I'd like to point out:

- Who's who in the IRC channel (`http://wiki.splunk.com/Community:IRC`).
- A list of things (mostly learned from experience) that we wish we knew when we started (`http://wiki.splunk.com/Things_I_wish_I_knew_then`).
- Enhancement requests—if you like what you see, open a support ticket and tell them as much. This is how we voice our opinions on how to make the software better (`http://wiki.splunk.com/Community:ERs`).

The content is changing all the time, so check out the Wiki from time to time.

User groups

User groups are important for Splunk. A user group is formed when a smaller region of Splunk users convene on their own to discuss, well, Splunk. It could be a city, a region of a state, or virtually any combination of users. For now, to find a user group, check out http://www.meetup.com and search for Splunk. Be on the lookout for the official Splunk user groups; they are coming soon. If you have questions on how to find a user group, write an e-mail to community@splunk.com with your questions.

The SplunkTrust

New for this year, the SplunkTrust is a formal recognition of community leaders. These are users who have contributed to the Splunk community in meaningful ways, be it answering questions on the answers website, leading a user group, submitting an App and supporting it, blogging, or catching a leprechaun. Any of these (and more, but probably not a leprechaun) would make you eligible for the program. Applications and nominations were accepted until the beginning of September, 2015. The members were announced at Splunk .conf 2015 during the induction ceremony. You will be able to identify the members; they will have a special icon on the answers website, and other places, that looks like a fez. If you see one of these members, feel free to approach them. We are here to help.

Summary

In this chapter, we went through the steps to publishing an App on Splunkbase. We made sure that our packaging was correct and that the initial verification steps were met. You learned about Splunk App certification, and how it can be beneficial to users and developers alike. After that, you learned about some places within the Splunk community in which you can find help, ask questions, discuss Splunk in detail, or just hang out.

Now you have reached the end of the book. We thank you for reading, and please let us know how we did (instructions for feedback are given in the *Preface*). After completing this book, you now have the required knowledge and insight into the world of Splunk application development. Be on the lookout for new and interesting ways to integrate with Splunk, and visit `http://dev.splunk.com` for more features and code in the future. Allons-y!

Index

Thank you for buying
Splunk Developer's Guide
Second Edition

About Packt Publishing

Packt, pronounced 'packed', published its first book, *Mastering phpMyAdmin for Effective MySQL Management*, in April 2004, and subsequently continued to specialize in publishing highly focused books on specific technologies and solutions.

Our books and publications share the experiences of your fellow IT professionals in adapting and customizing today's systems, applications, and frameworks. Our solution-based books give you the knowledge and power to customize the software and technologies you're using to get the job done. Packt books are more specific and less general than the IT books you have seen in the past. Our unique business model allows us to bring you more focused information, giving you more of what you need to know, and less of what you don't.

Packt is a modern yet unique publishing company that focuses on producing quality, cutting-edge books for communities of developers, administrators, and newbies alike. For more information, please visit our website at www.packtpub.com.

About Packt Enterprise

In 2010, Packt launched two new brands, Packt Enterprise and Packt Open Source, in order to continue its focus on specialization. This book is part of the Packt Enterprise brand, home to books published on enterprise software – software created by major vendors, including (but not limited to) IBM, Microsoft, and Oracle, often for use in other corporations. Its titles will offer information relevant to a range of users of this software, including administrators, developers, architects, and end users.

Writing for Packt

We welcome all inquiries from people who are interested in authoring. Book proposals should be sent to author@packtpub.com. If your book idea is still at an early stage and you would like to discuss it first before writing a formal book proposal, then please contact us; one of our commissioning editors will get in touch with you.

We're not just looking for published authors; if you have strong technical skills but no writing experience, our experienced editors can help you develop a writing career, or simply get some additional reward for your expertise.

Implementing Splunk

Second Edition

ISBN: 978-1-78439-160-7   Paperback: 506 pages

A comprehensive guide to help you transform Big Data into valuable business insights with Splunk 6.2

1. Learn to search, configure, and deploy Splunk on one or more machines.

2. Start working with Splunk fast, with a tested set of practical examples and useful advice.

3. Step-by-step instructions and examples with comprehensive coverage for Splunk veterans and newbies alike.

Mastering Splunk

ISBN: 978-1-78217-383-0   Paperback: 344 pages

Optimize your machine-generated data effectively by developing advanced analytics with Splunk

1. Develop simple applications into robust, feature-rich applications to search, monitor, and analyze machine-generated big data with ease.

2. Learn about lookups, indexing, dashboards, navigation, advances transaction with examples.

3. Understand the key features of Splunk by exploring real-world examples and apply the technology in your database.

Please check **www.PacktPub.com** for information on our titles

Splunk Essentials

ISBN: 978-1-78439-838-5   Paperback: 156 pages

Leverage the power of Splunk to efficiently analyze machine, log, web, and social media data

1. Make impressive reports and dashboards easily.

2. Search, locate, and manage apps in Splunk.

3. Use the Twitter app to create a dashboard based on Twitter searches of particular topics.

Splunk Operational Intelligence Cookbook

ISBN: 978-1-84969-784-2   Paperback: 414 pages

Over 70 practical recipes to gain operational data intelligence with Splunk Enterprise

1. Learn how to use Splunk to effectively gather, analyze, and report on the operational data across your environment.

2. Expedite your operational intelligence reporting, be empowered to present data in a meaningful way, and shorten the Splunk learning curve.

3. Easy-to-use recipes to help you create robust searches, reports, and charts using Splunk.

Please check **www.PacktPub.com** for information on our titles